WINNING AT THE GAME OF WIFE

WINNING
AT THE
GAME
OF
WIFE

How to Make Your Woman
Love You, Want You, & Adore You,
Like Never Before

JAMES T. HORNING

New York

WINNING AT THE GAME OF WIFE
How to Make Your Woman Love You, Want You,
& Adore You, Like Never Before

Published in New York, New York, by Morgan James Publishing. Morgan James and The Entrepreneurial Publisher are trademarks of Morgan James, LLC. www.MorganJamesPublishing.com

The Morgan James Speakers Group can bring authors to your live event. For more information or to book an event visit The Morgan James Speakers Group at www.TheMorganJamesSpeakersGroup.com.

Shelfie
A **free** eBook edition is available
with the purchase of this print book.

CLEARLY PRINT YOUR NAME ABOVE IN UPPER CASE
Instructions to claim your free eBook edition:
1. Download the Shelfie app for Android or iOS
2. Write your name in **UPPER CASE** above
3. Use the Shelfie app to submit a photo
4. Download your eBook to any device

ISBN 978-1-63047-674-8 paperback
ISBN 978-1-63047-675-5 eBook
Library of Congress Control Number:
2015909105

Cover Design by:
Rachel Lopez
www.r2cdesign.com

Interior Design by:
Bonnie Bushman
The Whole Caboodle Graphic Design

In an effort to support local communities and raise awareness and funds, Morgan James Publishing donates a percentage of all book sales for the life of each book to Habitat for Humanity Peninsula and Greater Williamsburg

Get involved today, visit
www.MorganJamesBuilds.com

DEDICATION

To my lovely wife, Kimberly, who exemplifies all the attributes of real love. She consistently gives me heavenly glimpses behind the veil of our humanity. Without her, I would not be the man I am today, and this book certainly would not exist. I love you Kimberly. You are my goddess and my muse!

To my daughter Bella who is still trying to help me unleash my 7 year old spirit. Thank you for choosing me to be your dad. I love you Baby Girl!

TABLE OF CONTENTS

ACKNOWLEDGMENTS

I want to acknowledge some of the great thinkers in the fields of psychotherapy, marriage coaching, and personal development who have influenced and helped to deepen my own thinking and understanding of the psychology, purpose, mystery, dynamic, and wondrous possibility within the marriage of a woman and a man. These remarkable individuals include Dr. David Schnarch, Dr. John Gottman, Dr. Wayne Dyer, Dr. John Gray, Esther Perel, Tony Robbins, Willard F. Harley Jr., David Deida and Mihaly Csikszentmihalyi. Many thanks for your groundbreaking work.

Thanks to everyone who read my rough drafts during the fine tuning of the manuscript. Your encouragement and personal testimonials helped drive me to the finish line. Many thanks to the editorial staff at SplitSeed for cleaning up my punctuation and verifying the accuracy of my quotes and references.

I want to thank my grandfather, Dr. MC Horning, for teaching me at an early age that women are smarter than men. Whether empirically true or not is not important. It has had a profound influence in the development of my high regard, honor and respect for them.

I want to thank my Uncle Phil for caring enough to point out destructive behavior to me early on in my marriage. Without his inadvertent blow to my ego, I may never have had the awareness to grow to where I am today.

Lastly, I want to thank my Mom for doing such a remarkable job raising me under often very challenging circumstances. My esteem for her largely influenced my early chivalrous approach to women of all ages.

SKEPTICS
READ THIS FIRST

Do I have to emasculate myself to be a "good husband"?
Heck no! This book is about what a "real" man does to bring
out his woman's inner goddess. A key ingredient to the equation
is supporting your inherent masculinity because guess what?
That's what attracted her to you in the first place. The manliest
thing a man can do is take care of his lady.

Is this going to be a lot of work? It doesn't have to be. I am
a strong believer in the Pareto Principle, otherwise known as the
80/20 Rule (very often it's the 90/10 rule). Pareto's law suggests
that 10 to 20 percent of what you do yields 80 to 90 percent of
your results. It's not how much you do that counts; it's what you
do and when you do it. Achieving outstanding results in your life
is more about psychology and knowing which screw to turn and

how much to turn it. This book is about learning distinctions that, once applied, have dramatic and immediate results. Every single chapter provides at least one profound takeaway that can turn your marriage around if applied wholeheartedly. And not once do I suggest that you need to talk more.

Is it possible to desire a woman you've lost attraction to? Once you understand the psychology of attraction, you'll know that the answer is a resounding YES. When you treat your lady like she is the object of your desire; when you daily let her know that she is your choice among all women; when you stop taking her for granted and make her feel pursued; when you start focusing on her qualities and not her faults—she will miraculously, over time, transform into a woman that you want. It is her nature to do so, and it's your job to draw it out.

When you change your own behavior for the better and lift yourself to a higher standard, you will pull your mate up with you. If you do it right, you'll have her wondering "Where have you been all my life?" However, it is a two-way street. If your mate has become someone who is unpleasant to be around and drags your quality of life into the gutter, the answer may be different.

What if she's lost attraction to me? Can I get it back? You bet! The principles above apply here as well. If she's lost attraction to you, then you have done one or more of the following: 1) you have lost polarity with her by somehow diminishing your masculine energy; 2) you are not meeting her needs on her terms; 3) she doesn't feel the significance of being the one daily chosen and pursued by you; 4) you've totally let yourself go, which sends her a signal suggesting that "If you can't take care of yourself, how are you going to take care of me?"—not to mention the fact that you're not very pleasant to look at; 5) you're just a total jerk and she has a negative association with you. What do you do now? You read this book from beginning to end and DO WHAT IT SAYS!

Is it too late to turn things around? That depends on your circumstances and how hurt, fed up, and disassociated your mate is. The answer in most cases is no, it is not too late. Oftentimes, no matter what your lady says, she is waiting for you to "man up" and come after her. And when you do, she may at first deny you to see if she is important enough for you to persist after. However, if you are one of those guys that got a note on the pillow in the morning saying, "I've had enough, I'm leaving you," then you better go straight to Chapter 8, Back from the Edge, and get your ass moving.

Is "good enough" good enough? And what if I'm content with how things are? If you were, you wouldn't have picked up this book. Besides, complacency is like leaving the keys to your woman's heart lying around. I am shocked at how many men I have known who woke up one morning to a note on their pillow saying something like, "I've had enough"; "I can't take it any longer"; "I'm leaving you"; or "It's over. Don't bother trying to fix it." It leaves the men reeling because, as they all say, "I didn't see it coming" or "I don't know what I did." Let me clue you in on something. It's not what you did. It's what you didn't do. If you think your marriage is "good," it's probably just "okay." If you think your marriage is "okay," I can guarantee you that trouble is lurking around the corner.

Is monogamy obsolete or even natural? Let me tell you guys that there is no greater pleasure than to have the all-out love, desire, and respect of a woman who worships you. There is an exhilarating freedom that comes in a relationship built on love, honor, respect, and trust. You are not only able to be who you really are, but you are supported in doing so by someone who has your back all the way. The notion that humans, anthropologically speaking, are not monogamous is irrelevant. Looking for insight into the nature of our sexuality by studying bonobo monkeys or philandering birds is demeaning at best. Researchers fail to acknowledge the one thing that really separates us from the animal kingdom: our minds. Cognitive thinking and the power of choice allow man to regulate, manipulate, and rule his own behavior.

One might argue that it is in the nature of man (or woman) to philander. I would argue that it is this same nature that compels us to lie, cheat, steal, and throw a tantrum if we don't get our way. Are we to reduce ourselves to the base nature of animals or live our lives to a higher God-given standard?

INTRODUCTION

How do you make your woman want you? By want you, I mean want YOU to be her man. I mean want to spend the rest of her life with you, knowing that you are the guy who fills all her needs and makes her feel like a woman. I mean want to connect with you in an emotional, physical, and spiritual way. I also mean want YOU in the most passionate and erotic sense. What's the one thing we all want and are willing to pay top dollar for? The answer is more. We want more. More money; more happiness; more fun; more excitement; more passion; more meaning; more love; and, yes, more sex. The game-changing magic that will bring more of these gifts into your life is about to be revealed. You will never see your wife or your marriage in the same way again. You're about to experience a paradigm shift that will change your life forever.

Caution!

This book is not for everybody. If you apply the information contained herein to yourself and your marriage, it's possible to have a "mind-blowing" relationship with your lover (wife). By mind-blowing, I mean an experience that far exceeds what most have ever witnessed or believed possible. Unfortunately, most people settle for mediocrity and are not willing to do what it takes to have an outstanding experience in their lives. If you're one of those people who gather information but don't put it into practice, **do not read this book!** I don't want you to spend the rest of your life feeling shortchanged, knowing what you could have had in your marriage.

If you've been married for any time at all, like me, you've probably wondered why the heck things aren't like they used to be. You may be asking: Where has the attraction gone? Where has the sex gone? Where is the passion we once had? Or maybe even: What has to happen to experience passion and a fulfilling life together that we've never had before? Or: How do we take our already good relationship to the stars?

Has "life" interfered with your ability to be intimate and have a healthy sex life? People get married for a few reasons, namely love, companionship, and, yes, sex. But somehow "everything" seems to screw the marriage up. Work, kids, health challenges, stress, deadlines—you name it. There are a hundred reasons why your relationship seems to take a backseat to the rest of your life. But I'm here to tell you that there is one BIG reason why you need to bring attraction and desire back into your marriage: YOUR MARRIAGE DEPENDS ON IT! AND THE QUALITY OF YOUR LIFE WILL HINGE ON THE QUALITY OF YOUR MARRIAGE.

This book is written for both men and women. I have written it for men in that, if they follow the principles I teach, they will certainly have a more fulfilling, passion-filled marriage. However, I have written it for women in that, if your man follows what I teach, he will become the husband of your dreams.

For me, marriage is the ultimate life experience. There is nothing more awesome than to witness the unveiling of the mystery that is a woman. And there is nothing more fulfilling than to experience her all-out love, honor, respect, and desire for you.

Whether you are newlyweds or marriage veterans, this book will show you what you need to do to create and nurture an environment where love and passion thrive. I'm going to give you powerful understanding and teach you the steps to take your relationship to new levels and your sexual connection to new heights.

What qualifies me to write this book? Well, I'm a very happily married man. In fact, I am crazy about my wife after twenty-seven years of marriage. I adore her, and she worships me (except on the rare occasion when I'm being an ass). I think a great marriage is the greatest gift that anyone can experience in life. Truth be known, I think I've got a really good thing going on. I've spent the last twenty years observing relationships, trying to understand and improve on the dynamics of my own, and reading the advice of experts in the field.

I'm not a sex therapist or a marriage counselor. I don't hold a degree in psychology. I'm just a regular guy who has spent years consciously dissecting his successes and failures as a husband. At one time or another I've been guilty of violating every single principle I teach in this book. But by perseverance and the good graces of my wife, the pendulum has swung from messing up 95 percent of the time to being a good husband 95 percent of the time, I think. For years I have offhandedly shared my "secrets to a great marriage" with people and have been often encouraged to write a book. But, ironically, the more I've learned, the less qualified I've felt to do it. However, after seeing so many marriages disintegrate and as many get stuck in sexless limbo, I felt compelled to do something about it.

My desire to impart quality information has led me to read more than ninety books by the best (and not so best) marriage counselors, relationship therapists, sex therapists, sexologists, and personal development coaches. I've attended high-priced seminars and workshops not only to grow my knowledge and understanding of this subject but to enhance the quality of my own relationship. During my research it became apparent that most therapists are not really "life experience" qualified to counsel couples, nor are the methodologies they practice efficacious. In other words, they don't know what they're talking about. Statistically, marriage counseling does not work.

So what does work? What are those mystical couples who are still in love after forty years doing that the rest are not? What is the blueprint for a great marriage? The answers to these questions will be revealed in the following pages using a variety of approaches—not just for reinforcement but because one paradigm will probably resonate with you better than another.

The understanding I've gained can be distilled into twelve insights that, if adopted as a code of conduct, will give you the relationship of your dreams. However, if you're a slow learner (when it comes to relationship stuff) as I am, a list of twelve things will not get you where you want to go. You need to have the psychology (inner game) that supports you in doing these things, because knowing and doing are two different things.

Once we've worked on the inner game, we'll attempt to demystify what it is that a woman wants; and, yes, there may actually be an answer to that eternal question.

The secret to a happy marriage is simple: find out what your woman wants and give it to her. End of story. Well, not really, but that's the super-duper, over-simplified version of the story. From there we'll explore the differences between men and women that drive you crazy and why crazy is good! And then, what the heck is a guy supposed to do? I mean, what is our job description? These mystical creatures did NOT come with a manual. Next, we'll dispel some of the myths people have about sex in marriage like Myth #2 that "great sex just doesn't happen in a monogamous relationship." And how do you bring sex back when it's not happening at all? And, finally, when the sex starts happening, how not to screw it up!

An important note to guys and gals: You will notice comment boxes like this one from time to time. These contain poignant remarks by my lovely wife, Kimberly. As much as I try to accurately represent a woman's needs and desires, I felt it important to include her insights and perspective to maintain the yin to my yang. I am eternally grateful for her love and have long realized that this book would not exist without her.

If you want access to more resources, or would like to get your hands on information in different media, I've got a plethora of FREE videos and articles online. Just go to **www. greatmarriagegreatlife.com** to watch, read or download free BONUS material. If you are committed to taking your relationship up a few notches, you will immerse yourself in everything you can get your hands on. Remember that knowledge isn't power. It is really just potential power. The power is in putting the knowledge into action. Having a support system in place is often a good way to make it across the chasm between where you are and where you want to be. Sometimes we can use a little prodding (i.e., kick in the ass) and I am here to be a real friend to you.

And finally, if you're not into reading books all the way through, feel free to skip around and grab hold of whatever resonates most with you and run with it. Every chapter stands on its own. However, all of it put together will give you the best results. I know it's said that "a little bit is better than nada," but if you can grab hold of the vision of marriage being the ultimate life experience, I think you'll want it all and be asking for more. If you turn yourself into the man of her dreams, she too will want it all and be asking for more.

CHAPTER 1

THE UNVEILING OF A WOMAN

Every woman is a mystery to be solved.
— From the movie ***Don Juan DeMarco***

Beyond Your Wildest Dreams

Ironically, this is the last chapter I'm writing. Sometimes it's hard to know where to start. Some say you start with the end in mind. Suffice it to say that if you do everything I share in this book and do it consistently, you will not only have more of your woman, you will have her in a way that will give you the ride of your life. The information I'm about share with you, when patiently implemented over time, will unleash the woman in your wife. If that sounds scary, it's not. It is, however, exhilarating and awe-inspiring, not unlike a ride at Disneyland, seeing the Tetons for the first time, or jumping out of an airplane.

Marriage is one of the great paradoxes of our time. What has been metaphorically referred to as "a ball and chain" and "the beginning of the end" is actually massively misunderstood, undervalued, and unappreciated. Marriage is life's greatest underutilized gift. Most married people don't know what they have. What would it be like if you were given Santa's bottomless toy bag but didn't know what you had? For most, marriage is like having a Ferrari in your garage that you use for a wheelbarrow. We really have no idea what we've got! We're bored, frustrated, and confused in the very presence of our panacea. Marriage is pure potentiality. If your marriage isn't giving you the time of your life, you're just not doing it right.

Since the beginning of time, men have, in hopeless confusion, tried to figure out what a woman wants. Stick with me as I give you a peek behind the veil at what could very well be your Avalon! I'll begin by reminding you of how wonderfully and beautifully women are made. Assuming you are a heterosexual male (and perhaps even if you're not), the facts below should inspire a new awe within you and serve to make everything in this book make sense and worth doing.

1. **Women are the most fascinating creatures on the face of this earth**. No other creature attracts and holds our attention like a woman. We love how they look, how they smell, how they feel, and how they drive us crazy. You know you love it! Their mystery and complexity

draws us in, fascinates us, and pushes us to our limits of comprehension and understanding. They are the yin to our yang. If you're fortunate enough to connect with your soul mate and are big enough (willing to grow and evolve as a human being) not to screw it up, you will be one of the fortunate few to have what I call "life's ultimate experience."

2. **Women have the gift of giving life.** Throughout history men have been capable of taking life. But anyone can do that. The gift that a woman has to bring a human being into existence is beyond compare. Our contribution is token at best. Their innate ability to conceive, grow, and birth a child is incomprehensible and has inspired reverential awe on one extreme and provoked fear and suppression on the other. Women are most deserving of our honor, respect, and worship.

3. **Women are God's mechanism for a man's ascension to "godliness."** (Don't worry, there's nothing religious about this book.) The process of becoming the "husband of her dreams" parallels the path to righteousness. Marriage is the ultimate growing experience. In striving to be the husband a woman deserves, a man is forced to overcome his carnal tendencies that are exacerbated in the presence of only men. In a man's complete and total pursuit of his woman, he learns what it truly means to love; he learns to surrender self; he learns mastery over his emotions; and in her unveiling, he witnesses those attributes that a woman exemplifies best, including patience, compassion, and tenderness. Blasphemous?

Hardly. Woman is man's perfect complement. She is the exemplification of everything that doesn't come natural to us.

4. **Women are the only creature to have an organ designed solely for experiencing pleasure.** Their sexuality is mystical. The pleasure they are capable of experiencing is incomprehensible to a man. They are the definition of sensuality. It's a myth that women are the "low-desire" partner. As you will learn later, there's a big difference between sex drive and desire.

5. **Women are the inspiration and motivation behind all progress.** A university professor of mine surmised that, historically, all exploration, innovation, and progress was inspired or motivated by man's desire and need to attract women or impress women. I don't know how true this is historically, but I do know that I wouldn't be the man I am now, or have achieved what I have, without the inspiration and provocation of the woman in my life.

6. **Women are sensual creatures.** A woman's nature is sensuality exemplified. Their sensuality comes through when they're allowed by circumstance to express their true nature; when they can feel like a woman, think like a woman, express themselves like a woman, and act like a woman. A woman's mind, body, and spirit can combine to make the experience of her love and sexuality truly transcendental. They also can combine to make your life a living hell. This duality is one of life's great paradoxes. A woman's

latent potential for witchery and bitchcraft is rivaled only by a man's potential for unthinkable and dastardly deeds.

Women and men both reside in, as Deepak Chopra puts it, the field of pure potentiality. In short this means that the potential exists for anything to manifest itself given the right conditions of intention, expectation, and environment. Basically, this means that you manifest your own heaven and hell. You do the math.

So that's what this book is all about: learning what has to happen to unveil the woman that is inside your wife. If what I've described is not something you're experiencing, it's because she has been miseducated, mistreated, suppressed, and/or her needs have not been met. If your woman doesn't desire you or want sex, or the sex just isn't great anymore, somewhere along the line you or someone else has really messed her up, and it's your job as her husband to create an environment where her true nature can blossom. It will require you to dig deep and be more of a man than you ever have been.

We're going to start this ride off by finding out once and for all "what a woman wants" and then get into the inner game of being the man she deserves. All the principles in this book apply to both men and women, so ladies, if you're reading, don't think this stuff applies only to your man.

I want to reiterate a statement made in the Introduction: *For me, marriage is the ultimate life experience. There is nothing more awesome than witnessing the unveiling of the mystery that is a woman. And there is nothing more fulfilling than experiencing her all-out love, honor, respect, and desire for you.*

This is what it's all about, guys. Sex is important. Really important! However, it's just a part of a larger canvas. Experiencing life with a woman by your side is the greatest gift there is. All experiences are magnified when shared with someone else, especially someone of the opposite sex. When you learn to be the man that she deserves, you will experience what can only be described as heaven on earth.

THE TWELVE INSIGHTS
(OK. It's really 13)

This chapter is for you guys that can't seem to get past Chapter 1 of a self-help book, which I sincerely hope is not the case. Here are my twelve insights that, if sincerely and devoutly followed, will help to pave your way to marital bliss. They embody all the principles in this book. I encourage you to read them, reread them, meditate on them, and do them; then read them, meditate on them, and do them ad infinitum. But please don't stop here. It only gets better.

1. **Love, honor, respect, and worship the woman in your life.** Treat her like she is the woman of your dreams. Learn to ask the following questions of yourself in the moments when you know in your gut that your behavior will drive a wedge between you and

your woman. Is this making my woman feel loved? Will she feel more honored and respected as a result of my words or actions? Is this an act of devotion and worship? If your "loving" actions will not increase your woman's emotional and physical desire for you, you can trust that they are not in the true spirit of love, honor, and respect.

2. **Always remember that as *right* as you think you are, you may be and frequently *are* completely wrong.** A corollary to this is to relinquish the need to be right. Needing to be right and always "prove it" is egocentric, selfish, narcissistic, and ignorant. And it is a fast track to ruining a relationship and developing a cold bed. Do you want to be "right", or do you want to be loved, honored, and respected?

3. **Let go of the need to "understand."** You may never understand why your wife does some of the things she does and thinks some of the things she thinks. It's okay! It's part of her being who she is, a woman. Another way of saying this is to relinquish the need to make sense of everything. The more you try to make sense of something your wife does or says, the greater the emotional chasm that forms between you.

4. **Just because you think it, doesn't mean you should say it.** Read it again! I personally say things quite frequently that I shouldn't say to my wife, but I'm getting better at censoring it before it comes out of my mouth. Contrary to what most of us believe, saying to your wife, "You would look really good

in that dress if you could fit into it," is NOT an affirmation of how good you think she looks. To her, you just said she is fat! When she has made you fifteen minutes late to an appointment for the seven thousandth time saying, "Your inconsideration of other people's time is an embarrassment to me," is totally counterproductive—no matter what you think. All she hears is that she is an embarrassment to you. Here's a rule of thumb. Before you open your mouth, play the whole tape starting with why you are about to say what you want to say (likely it is for reasons of personal gain or ego); visualize how your lady is likely to respond based on your past experience; and finally, ask yourself what good will come of it. If your lady's likely response is, "Baby, you're the best! I can't wait to make love to you tonight!" then you know you're on the right track. If her likely response is to feel hurt, demeaned, belittled, distanced, unappreciated, or unloved, then you know that you are about to f**k up.

5. **Assume that your wife is at least as smart as you.** Whether she is or isn't is something you will never really know because you see everything from a male perspective. However, if you treat her "as if," she will get more of the respect, honor, and significance that she well deserves. My grandfather "Pappy" taught me this when I was a kid. He said, "The sooner you learn that women are smarter than men, the better off you'll be." Pappy was a very smart man.

6. **Do your share around the house.** This is particularly important in a dual-income household. Take your share of the load, and then some. That's the manly thing to do. In fact, statistically, one of the biggest complaints of women in unsatisfying marriages is that they don't get enough help around the house. Don't be a statistic.

7. **Tell her you love her, show her you love her, tell her you love her, show her you love her, tell her you love her, show her you love her ad infinitum.** Get it? This is your life's work. The key here is to do it on her terms, not yours. That means you need to learn what makes her feel loved, and sometimes the only way to do this is to ask her. What a thought! When she feels loved, she's much more receptive and proactive sexually.

8. **Buy her a horse.** Don't freak out. You don't have to buy her a horse, although it's not a bad idea. Figuratively speaking, this means to give her the gift of consistent re-creation—an activity, hobby, or place she can go to rebuild and rejuvenate herself physically, emotionally, and spiritually. We all need a respite from the daily grind. Guys tend to retreat to the TV, garage, golf course, or_____ [you fill in the blank]. Your lady needs this too.

9. **Know, understand, and support her dream(s).** Your dreams are important and so are hers. Make sure she knows that even if your present circumstances don't support her dream(s), they are important to you and won't be forgotten. You want to ensure that her life with you represents not a big compromise but a joint-

venture in enthusiastically supporting each other's "thing that they need to do." They don't have to be mutually exclusive.

10. **Give her security.** A woman needs to feel safe, secure, and protected. Don't ever allow her to be in a position where she's insecure about your financial well-being or your love for her. Money worries stress a woman's femininity and compromise her need for things to be "all right." And when things aren't "all right" with momma, they're not right for anybody. Additionally, insecurity over your love and connection with her diminishes her desire for sex. Take away any doubt that she is the woman in your life.

11. **Eliminate negativity.** Negativity is anything you say or do that makes your mate feel negative. It doesn't matter whether you think something is negative or not. All that matters is what your mate thinks. Negativity can show up in facial expressions or tone of voice. It's not what you say sometimes but how you say it. Negativity can be felt in sarcasm, condescension, and joking. It's easy to say something hurtful and then say you were just joking. Criticism, no matter how "constructive," is usually perceived negatively. Bottom line: if she doesn't like it, don't do it! If you know deep down that something you are doing or saying is making her feel bad, don't do it! The last thing you want is for your mate to have a negative association with you. When you walk into the room, does she light up like a Christmas tree or give you a look that says, "What

in hell are you doing here?" If your woman develops a negative association to your face, your presence, your voice, or whatever—you will lose her. Guaranteed. If she doesn't legally separate herself from you, she will most certainly separate herself from you emotionally and either consciously or subconsciously look to have her needs for love and significance met elsewhere.

12. **Romance her.** A woman wants and needs romance. It nurtures and releases her femininity. It makes her feel like a woman again. In an age of dual-income families and career-oriented women, ladies are often competing in a "man's world" doing work in an environment that doesn't support feminine virtues. Romance gives her a chance to be a woman and stay in touch with her feminine side. It brings the polarity back into a relationship that is essential for sexual attraction.

13. **Bring Your "A-Game."** This may be the most important concept of all because if you don't have on your "A-game," you are powerless to implement the preceding eleven insights. What I mean by A-game is consistently being in an empowering peak state of mind and learning to access that state at will. If you are in an empowered, resourceful, and grateful state of mind, it is easy to be loving, understanding, positive, respectful, thoughtful, supportive, and romantic. It is nearly impossible for you to exhibit these attributes if you are not. Learning to master your emotions and enter an empowering peak state at will is a skill that

lies at the very foundation of your success in love and in life.

Okay, that's all good, but don't stop here. You've obviously come this far because you're a man who wants your lady to have the love and the life she deserves. It's not enough to learn these principles conceptually. You want the tools and understanding to make it a reality in your life, so let's get after it.

 **Takeaways**

Just do it!

CHAPTER 2

AN ACT OF DESPERATION

"Don't leave!"
    —The secret to staying married for a long time
    as told to Chris Isaak (music artist) by his mother.

Modern marriage is a travesty. Travesty is often defined as a grotesque or absurd misrepresentation of a truth or reality or even an inferior imitation of something more profound. Marriage, as most know it, is very shallow and superficial. Most people have never explored its depths. In fact, most people are completely unaware of its infinite layers. How could we know? Our initiation into married life is given to us by the often dysfunctional examples of our parents, relatives, friends, and society at large. It's ironic that the most significant decision and commitment we will make in life comes without any real preparation or education. The fact is that most of us have no clue what the heck we're doing!

Consider for a moment what makes up the bulk of our lives, namely our careers, our special interests (hobbies), and our marriage. We commit significant amounts of time and energy into growing our skills to make ourselves more valuable and competitive in the workplace and on the golf course, for example. We pursue higher education, participate in workshops, go to seminars, and engage in continuing education so that we can excel in our jobs, make more money, and be more significant. What if we put the same amount of heart and focus into mastering the nuances of love and marriage as we put into getting a trout to rise to our hand-tied Caddis fly? Why does it not occur to us that, just maybe, we need to go to school and learn exactly how to be married and be a good husband? What would happen if we put the same energy into our relationship with our woman that we put into learning how to take our careers to the next level?

I'll tell you what would happen. You might just discover that the woman in your life is your greatest gift and that your marriage might just be your life's greatest experience. If conversations with your lady aren't inspiring and the sex isn't mind-blowing, you just aren't doing it right. I discovered this the hard way like most men do. If you're anything like me, you might need to get knocked upside the head with a two-by-four before you realize that you're a little rough around the edges.

Now, whenever I am with my beautiful wife, I know that I am the luckiest man in the world. My deep love, attraction, and desire for her is mirrored by her deep love, attraction, and desire for me. I mean, she really wants me. She wants me because I inspire her, stimulate her mind, and fill her needs for love at a high level, among other things. But it wasn't always this way.

As I write this, I'm thinking back to a time about fifteen years ago when our "good" marriage wasn't as solid as I thought; back when I was pretty ignorant of what my woman's needs were and was more concerned about meeting my own. Sound familiar? We've always had a good marriage, but my skills at being a good husband were pretty sorrowful in contrast to where I am today. I have to thank God for my wife's untiring love, patience, and belief in me.

Back in the old days, when my wife and I were engaged in an argument or debate, my desire to be "right" and prove my point overrode any desire I had for my wife to feel loved and respected. What a jerk I was! One day we were driving up a canyon near our home. I don't remember the topic of discussion but I do remember that it got very heated. In fact, our negative emotions were ridiculously disproportionate to the low significance of the subject matter. Ever been there? I'm certain we disagreed over something that had no bearing on anything that really matters. After all, what can be more important than your marriage? What can be more important than being at peace with your mate?

Well, at the time I thought being right was more important than being happily married. In fact, my insistence that we continue to argue a petty point until she came over to my way of thinking drove my wife to desperation—desperation to relieve herself of my presence. She screamed at me to stop the car so she could get out. Upon my refusal, she flung the car door open and convincingly moved to throw her body from the vehicle. I slammed on the brakes while pulling over to the side of the road. This all seemed to happen in one single motion. Beyond running down the side of the road after my wife, the rest is a blur. However, it was a defining experience for me, one that ultimately inspired my determination and journey to be the husband she deserves.

A couple of weeks later, I was listening to Wayne Dyer on CD while driving down the highway. I think it was his book Real Magic. He shared one of many concepts that have influenced my life tremendously, but on this day the concept could not have been more poignant. He told a story of how relinquishing the need to be right changed his life and made it so much easier to have harmony in a relationship.

I immediately adopted the concept, and without delay it became a new behavioral pattern for me. Relinquishing the need to be right does not come without its challenges because it is an ego-driven habit of behavior. The trick is to get leverage on yourself. A technique that has worked well for me and many of my coaching clients is to premeditate how you are going to handle yourself the next time you are in a situation where your need to be right or where getting in the last word usually takes over. Consciously choose your lady and your marriage over everything else. Consciously acknowledge to yourself that your mate's peace, happiness, and well-being are paramount over your desire to satisfy an ego-driven urge for significance. Visualize the dire consequences of your mate consistently feeling insignificant or belittled and how that could translate into the future. Fully associate yourself with the pain you will experience if you don't change this behavior. If that's not enough, fully associate with the pain you might be causing your lady by consistently disrespecting her individuality. Ask yourself the question: Does this behavior make my mate feel loved? If the answer is no, then doing it is destructive to your relationship. Period.

Relinquishing the need to be right was a huge turning point in my marriage. Allowing my wife to disagree with me and honoring her unique points of view was a liberating experience. In the long run it also has saved eating a lot of crow. As often as I "knew" empirically that I was right, with time I discovered that I was sometimes wrong. How ignorant it is, I've learned, to ignore a woman's equally valid perspective on things—even when it seems incomprehensible to you. All said, my wife's desire to throw herself from a moving vehicle was an eye-opener for me. I realized that she deserved much more than I was then equipped to give her. I needed some education. I needed to grow as a man and as a human being. I needed to learn to love her on her terms instead of my own. Without her, I never would have developed into the man I am today. I would have had no compelling reason.

Making mistakes and correcting them is one of the greatest modes for personal growth. If your answer to facing challenges in your marriage is to flake out and say, "That's just the way I am" or "She/he needs to just accept me for who I am," then you're denying yourself of your personal power to grow, mold, and shape your own mind. This approach suggests that you are satisfied with stagnation and complacency. It's a total copout! What comes natural or easy to us may be counterproductive, destructive, and non-supportive of a great relationship. I can personally testify that adopting new perspectives, thought patterns, and habits of response is a necessary step in the path to being the husband your wife deserves.

More recently I had an extremely rare "blowup" directed at my wife. She had given me a look that conjured up a bad memory for me. My response was completely disproportionate to the moment because I was reacting to my own hallucination of what was not a current reality. The worst part was that it happened in front of our seven-year-old daughter. Later that day, as I was helping my little girl get ready for bed, I apologized to her for what had happened earlier that day. Her response blew me away. She said matter-of-factly, as she was brushing her teeth, "Daddy, we should just let other people think what they want to think and want what they want." Out of the mouths of babes... Which leads me to the question: What does a woman want?

♥ Takeaways ♥

1. Most of us have only a superficial concept of what marriage is supposed to be and no idea of its wonderful possibilities.

2. Our marriage deserves the same level of focus, attention, and education that we typically put into our careers and hobbies. What would happen if we actually learned how to be the husband our wife deserves?

3. Relinquishing the need to be right or the need to understand can be a huge turning point in your marriage.

4. As my daughter so wisely suggested, we need to let people just be who they are and not try to change them. There is a word for that: RESPECT.

CHAPTER 3

WHAT A WOMAN WANTS–REALLY!

> *The great question that has never been answered and which I have not been able to answer, despite my thirty years of research into the feminine soul, is, "What does a woman want?"*
>
> **—Sigmund Freud**

She Wants What She Wants

My daughter, when she was three, epitomized the sentiment of all women when she was crying and I asked, "Sweet Pea, what do you want?" Her reply: "Daddy, I want what I want." My internal response was: What the heck does that mean? I can't believe she's already dishing out this mind-scrambling stuff! What blows my mind is that her response was not learned or cultivated. It was innate. It came natural because it was her nature. And we've all heard the old adage that you don't mess with Mother Nature.

Further proving the nature of my daughter's statement, I want to share with you The Legend of Dame Ragnelle. The earliest version of this tale is found in The Canterbury Tales by Geoffrey Chaucer; however, the following retelling is a considerably shortened (for your sake) paraphrasing by my lovely wife Kimberly.

One day King Arthur is hunting for deer in the forest when he is ambushed by a knight with an old grievance against him and intending to take his life. The knight agrees to spare his life in exchange for answering one of the world's greatest mysteries: "What does a woman want?" He gives the king one year to discover the answer.

The king immediately returns to his court and solicits the help of his most trusted knight. Over the course of a year together they question every man and woman in the land with no satisfactory answer.

As his deadline approaches the king once again returns to the forest on another hunt, but this time he encounters an old hag, Dame Ragnelle. A grotesque hunchbacked woman, her "nose is snotted withal and through her yellow protruding teeth" she tells King Arthur she knows the answer to the age-old question but will only reveal the truth if his knight, Sir Gawain, will agree to take her hand in marriage.

The king immediately seeks Sir Gawain's consent to Dame Ragnelle's proposition, which he gives: "I will wed her at what time you will set," he says to his king. "For love of you I will not hesitate."

When the king returns to Dame Ragnelle and shares Sir Gawain's approval, she reveals the answer: "What women most want is the power to choose for themselves."

After the wedding between Dame Ragnelle and Sir Gawain, the knight kisses his new bride and she is immediately transformed into a beautiful young woman—"The fairest creature that ever he saw without measure." She explains that she was under a curse, "transformed by necromancy into a hunchbacked old crone until a courteous knight like you married and kissed me." The newly married couple "made mirth in the bedroom all night."

In the morning the beautiful maiden explains that the curse is only partially lifted. "But it is not fully lifted. Because of you I am now free to be my true beautiful self…but only for half the day! My beauty will not hold. So I must ask you, dear husband, which do you choose? To have me beautiful by day and ugly in the night, or beautiful by night and ugly in the day?"

"I don't know what to do," Sir Gawain says. "Choose what you think best, dear lady. The choice I put into your hand. Do as you want."

Dame Ragnelle responds, "Thank you, dear husband. Now you have lifted the whole curse. Because you gave me the choice, you shall have me beautiful both day and night, always fair and bright. Because you gave me the power to choose what I want instead of what you want, you've freed me to be my beautiful self always."

Well, what do you know? Just as my little girl said, a woman wants what she wants—meaning she doesn't want your preferences shoved down her throat. She wants to be able to choose her own course. Is this all she wants? I don't think so. It couldn't possibly be that simple. So let's begin to move in the direction of grasping this unfolding mystery of what a woman wants. First, let's divide the wants of a woman into two distinct categories: tangible wants and intangible wants.

Tangible Wants

Tangible wants are those things that we as men should know about but are too stupid or insensitive to recognize. Our wives expect us to intuit these things and don't think they should have to tell us. However, they frequently leave us clues that we often don't pick up on because we're too self-absorbed in our own needs.

We're supposed to observe with sensitivity. We're expected to perform investigative research to identify what these things are and provide them at just the right time—and many of them all the time. Some are quite obvious and some require a little sleuthing. But don't you get it? That's what they want! They want to be pursued. They like being a mystery to be solved. They want you to figure these things out on your own. It helps them know you care. You might say, "Gee, I did all that stuff when we were dating or when we first got married. She knows I care. I told her twelve years ago." You idiot! She needs to be courted foreverrrrrrrrr.

If she sees that you care enough, that she's significant enough for you to continue exploring her wants, needs, and desires, and you keep actively filling them—I'm telling you guys, your lady will worship and adore you.

When you read the word "want", I want you to also see the word "need" because most of what a woman wants is really an unfulfilled need. By need I mean that she actually needs these things to feel loved by you, to feel secure in her relationship with you, to feel attracted to you, and to feel like a whole human being. You might be thinking Gee, this is a lot of stuff, but guess what? You have your own version of the same wants (needs), so get over it. If you really think about it, these wants are quite obvious. The problem is that most guys don't really think about it. So here's the obvious list of what she wants in no particular order.

- ❤ Financial security
- ❤ Significance
- ❤ Love
- ❤ Romance
- ❤ Affection
- ❤ Appreciation
- ❤ Focused attention

- ❤ Loving gestures
- ❤ Fun with you
- ❤ Time for herself
- ❤ Help with the housework
- ❤ Respect
- ❤ Honor
- ❤ Flowers once in a while
- ❤ Surprises
- ❤ Great sex (yes, she wants it too)
- ❤ A man, not a wuss
- ❤ To feel beautiful
- ❤ To feel worthy of being pursued
- ❤ To be listened to and really heard
- ❤ For you to be the guy who represented you when you were courting

This last one is explored further later on, but it deserves equal time here because a lot of women feel like they were sold a bill of goods. Meaning, you never really showed her all of the real you when you were dating. What she saw was the "salesman" side of you. You were trying to sell yourself. A salesman only points out the sellable features. He accentuates the positive. We all do. She did too. However, you might consider putting a little more polish on yourself and a little less on the sports car or motorcycle you have in the garage. And as for the "real you," maybe he could use a little work. Saying, "That's just the way I am," is a copout. If your car has plugged injectors, you clean them out! If your business isn't cash flowing, you cut costs and work on your sales and customer service. Right? Well, if you're not being a good husband, maybe you need some overhauling too. Just a thought.

What she wants is to experience the YOU that made her fall in love with you. Actually, she deserves an improved version of who she met. It only seems fair that as a growing and evolving human being, which I know you are, that your mate can expect growth and improvement in the "husbanding" department.

The above list is pretty universal. But don't assume that's all there is. Your woman may have wants that can only be uncovered by doing something that would never occur to most men—asking her.

>>>—♥→

It's not enough to just ask her. You need to truly want to know her answer. If you don't truly want to know, act as if you do.

Here are some questions that will help you get to the bottom of what your woman wants:

- Honey, what can I do to take a load off you?
- Sweetie, what would make your day today?
- Baby, what feels best? When I do this or when I do this?
- Muffin, because I am crazy about you, I want to know what makes you feel loved. I also want to know what

I might do that makes you feel unloved so I can stop doing that.

- Love of my life, I want to know what your hopes and dreams are, because I want to help make them a reality.

If you make not listening a habit, she will stop telling you what she wants and stop giving you clues.

A Gentle Warning

When asking these questions, be prepared for the backlash of "I've been trying to tell you these things for seven years now and you've been too blockheaded [or selfish, self-centered, dumb, blind, stupid, idiotic, etc.] to hear me!"

You see, right up to the time that we're supposed to "magically" know what our woman wants, or read her mind, we've probably been given about ten thousand hints that we were too blind to see.

A woman feels loved and respected when little things are heeded. This acknowledges that her voice is heard when she says things like, "Honey, please put the toilet seat down when you're finished. I know this is a pain in the tail, and you wonder why I shouldn't leave it up for you, but you've never stumbled into the bathroom at three a.m. and sat down on a sticky, cold, ceramic rim." Get it?

Intangible Wants

You know, the funny thing is that a guy "wants what he wants" too. The difference is that he generally knows what he wants and then goes and gets it. A woman "wants what she wants" but doesn't always know what that is until she's shopped all day for it. (Hint to the guys: What she wants is to shop. It's like fishing. It's not so much about catching fish as it is about just "fishing." Hint to the gals: For a guy, shopping all day in the same department of the same store is a mind-altering experience. Think scrambled eggs.]

So, if she doesn't know what she wants, how in hell is a guy supposed to know what she wants? The answer is he's not! You're not supposed to know. This, my friends, is one of the things that drives men mad. But here's the truth of the matter. If she was like you, you never would have been attracted to her. If what she wanted was predictable, you'd be bored out of your mind. She's a girl. She's your counterpart, your equal but opposite. From a mechanical design perspective, what sense does it make having to squat to pee? If you're wearing pants, it requires you to expose your entire tail end and, if in the outdoors, make yourself very vulnerable to snakebite (speaking from personal experience as an observer). Would you prefer she had a penis? I don't think so! They're not called the opposite sex for nothing.

I hope you all can see that I'm half joking here, but every good joke has a poignant truth at its core. Sometimes it seems that a woman's wants are a moving target, at best vague and unclear. But that's only because they don't always say what they really mean, nor do they always really want direct answers to the questions they ask. Like me, you might be thinking WTF!

A quintessential example of this is when she notices her man is troubled; she asks if he would like to talk about it. She does this because that's what she would want him to do for her. A man will usually say no. What he means by no is "No, I don't want to talk about it." If a man notices his wife is troubled, and he's an insensitive jerk, he will avoid asking her anything because he doesn't want to open up an emotional can-of-worms (translation: he cares more about his needs than her needs). If he is half a man, he will ask her if anything is bothering her and whether she would like to talk about it. She will probably say no and may even resist any advance he initially makes to talk.

At this point most guys are like, Thank God, I really didn't want to get into anything emotional anyway. She's the one who doesn't want to talk, so I'm off the hook. But a woman almost always wants to talk. So what she really means by all this is that she wants to be pursued and coaxed. This shows her that you care, are genuinely interested, and that she's worth pursuing. Please note that there are infinite permutations of the above dynamic and many exceptions that are covered in other sections of the book. For example, a guy doesn't always get what he wants because he isn't comfortable expressing his feelings, needs, or desires. He might want a blowjob once in a while but doesn't want to risk rejection or be made to feel selfish in asking. Well, what do you know. Guys have feelings too!

She Doesn't Want What She Wants! Huh?

Now we're having fun. If you're anything like me you've been driven crazy by a woman's infinite capacity to change her mind. What she wants is often a moving target. A woman with a feminine core is governed by feeling, emotion, mood, and spontaneity. Sometimes what she needs is for you to step up and make decisions for her. Decisiveness is a strongly masculine trait. Her indecisiveness is an exemplification of her femininity.

Often your woman will look to you to demonstrate your masculinity through objectivity and decisiveness. When she asks for your opinion on something and your response is "Make yourself happy…do whatever you want," you think you are saying the right thing, but in fact you are undermining your masculinity and she feels it. As much as a woman "wants what she wants," what she wants most is for you to support the polarity between her femininity and your masculinity. She wants to know that you are a man. Show her that you are in control of a situation while supporting her ability to choose for herself; this demonstrates that she can trust you to take care of her.

Sometimes she doesn't really want what she says she wants. What she's doing is testing you to see if you will be man enough to be true to yourself and your higher purpose. Women often consciously and unconsciously look for evidence that supports your masculinity. She may say that she wants you to stay home and snuggle all day in bed, but she would probably lose respect and attraction for you if you did.

>>>💗→

Sometimes what we ask for is a test; a desire to see your response, your commitment, your support, or your love. We don't always necessarily want or have to have what we ask for. We just want to know that you are willing to give it to us.

A lot of things about a woman seem incomprehensible to a man. Did it ever occur to you that she may feel the same way about you? The best thing you can do is surrender your need to understand and embrace the unfolding mystery that is your wife. What is not a mystery, however, is that there are six fundamental human needs (covered in another chapter) that we all have whether you are consciously aware of them or not. When you gain an understanding of these needs and seek to help your partner meet them, the intangible wants become tangible manifestations of fulfilled desire.

If this all looks like a lot of work, just remember this: the manliest thing a man can do is take care of his woman and provide for her every need. The rewards for this are immeasurable and result in an extraordinary relationship that is truly life altering and cannot be fully described in words.

This chapter can be summed up in the words of a new song by country music artist Julia Burton: "A woman wants a man who...doesn't have to be told what a woman wants." I'm going to take it a step further. **"A woman wants a man who knows what she wants and takes pleasure in giving it to her."**

♥ Takeaways ♥

1. Find out what your woman wants and give it to her. It may not make any sense to you. It may not be logical. It doesn't matter. What does matter is that it matters to her.

2. Remember that your wants are not necessarily her wants.

3. She needs to be courted forever. She needs to know that you are choosing her on a daily basis. To her, the courting process is evidence of this. It is an affirmation to her that she is "the one" you have chosen.

4. She wants you to know what she wants without having to tell you. Knowing what she wants is evidence that you have been focused on her and present with her. After all, if you are truly "present" when you are with her, you will know what she wants because she drops a thousand hints a day whether she knows it or not.

Practice the art of listening. This means being present and focused on your mate while they are expressing themselves. This is one of the greatest gifts you can give. And don't just hear the words but also feel the underlying message being communicated.

CHAPTER 4

WOMEN ARE CRAZY AND MEN ARE STUPID

Women are smarter than men. The sooner you learn this the happier you'll be.

— **Dr. Merritt Horning** as told to his grandson Tad

Mars and Venus

John Gray in his bestselling book Men Are from Mars, Women Are from Venus uses the Mars and Venus metaphor to help us understand the differences between men and women. The metaphor illustrates the extreme and often incomprehensible differences in the way men and women think, communicate, and love. As helpful and insightful as Dr. Gray's message has been, I prefer to view men and women as two sides of the same coin, the quintessential yin and yang of the universe, perhaps even the two faces of God personified in human beings. There is no finer complement in the universe than a man and woman.

So stop trying to change each other. We're supposed to be different. The extreme differences between us are what attract us together in the beginning but seem to drive us crazy in this thing we call marriage. Most relationship problems come from men and women thinking and acting like we're the same. We're clearly not! Get over it and embrace it! Let's look at a few obvious differences. Some you're probably cool with and others you would like to change but shouldn't.

1. You're male; she's female.
2. You've got a penis; she has a vagina (just wanted to clear up any ambiguity).
3. You pee standing up; she does it sitting down.
4. You're mono-orgasmic, she's multiorgasmic.
5. You have pecs; she has breasts.
6. You have strength; she has softness.
7. You like to kill things; she likes to nurture things.
8. You like to grill; she likes to bake.
9. You think objectively; she thinks subjectively.
10. She can have babies; you can't (good thing too; you couldn't handle the pain).
11. She bleeds once a month; you don't (and thank God you don't because you'd probably be running to the ER every time it happened).

12. You like the bed firm; she likes it soft.

13. She likes to talk about her feelings; you don't want feelings.

14. She shops; you buy.

15. You want to feel like a hero; she wants to be rescued.

16. You need to understand why; she just "wants what she wants."

17. You are logical; she is intuitive.

18. You think she's crazy; she thinks you're stupid.

19. You like craft beer; she likes California White Zinfandel.

20. You use sex as a way of reconnecting with your partner; she wants to reconnect before she has sex.

21. You're a microwave; she's a Crock-Pot. You can get aroused just looking at a naked woman. She gets aroused by feeling secure, loved, romanced, nurtured, focused on, sexy, kissed, touched, tantalized…etc. Just a note about Crock-Pots: If you keep them turned on, they will always be hot.

22. You think fly fishing on a remote lake in Saskatchewan that takes you three days to reach by canoe is a vacation. She thinks vegan cooking classes followed by yoga and a facial at Canyon Ranch Spa is a vacation.

23. You're five minutes in the bathroom; she's an hour.

24. She takes small problems and makes them as big as possible; you pretend big problems are less significant than they really are.

25. You need a reason for everything; she gives you the reason.

26. You want to be inspired; she's your inspiration.

By now you're thinking yeah, we're total f**king opposites. You're darn right you are, and you want to keep it that way. But you know what? It's really cool! What we're talking about here is **polarity**. Polarity is opposite poles attracting each other. Polarity is what enamors you to the opposite sex. It's what instigates the infatuation and euphoria experienced in courtship. Polarity keeps you coming back for more. It's the "Can't live without 'em" part of the old adage we all know by heart. However, if you implement the principles in this book, the "You can't live with 'em" part will change. Polarity is what makes a marriage passionate. Polarity, and the sex you have as a result of it, is the primary thing that makes marriage different from all other relationships. Without passion and sex, all you have is a contractual "working" relationship. There are exceptions to this rule, but they are rare.

Here is a good place to throw in a little disclaimer. It's important to understand that I am primarily writing this book in a masculine voice to a masculine audience. I make generalizations about the dynamics and polarity between men and women that apply to roughly 80 percent of relationships. If you are one of the 10 to 20 percent of men who are more feminine in nature, the rules and principles still apply, just in reverse. There is almost always a predominantly masculine and predominantly feminine figure in any marriage. However, they do not always fall into traditional roles as we know them. My point is that this does not in any way discount the significance of maintaining a healthy polarity in your relationship. The old cliché that opposites attract is oh so true.

So what happens? Why do a man and woman (total opposites) fall in love and then get frustrated with their differences, fight over their differences, and often get divorced over their differences? The answer is simple. They don't realize that their differences (i.e., problems) are often actually blessings in disguise and evidence that they are probably perfectly compatible. They don't understand, appreciate, embrace, and nurture their polarity. Men and women are like vinegar and oil, distinctly different. One is acidic and harsh, the other smooth and silky. However, when combined, they complement each other perfectly. When emulsified with real love, they are inseparable. This emulsification happens when real love is demonstrated through filling your partner's six human needs, which will be discussed in Chapter 6.

A big problem, however, is that in today's two-income-family model, it's difficult to have polarity when he and she are both career oriented and take turns with the kids, meals, dishes, etc. In this scenario, polarity is lost because the lines between traditional roles have become blurred. The blurring of the lines between sexes is epidemic. Women are wearing pantsuits to the office in traditionally masculine roles while men are staying at home and going to yoga.

The ugly truth of the matter is that women's and men's natures support more traditional roles and not so much contemporary ones. As this book is not a treatise on human nature, I am speaking in generalizations. History, anthropology, social studies, and current surveys prove this. Men, generally speaking, are attracted to women who exhibit feminine qualities and features. They want a woman who looks healthy and fertile with an hourglass figure. Am I right? Men prefer a woman who makes them feel manly; a woman they feel they can protect and be a hero for.

In contrast, most women innately want a man they perceive can provide for them, take care of them, and protect them. They want a guy who is strong and capable. They want a man who makes them feel like a woman. Am I stereotyping men and women? Most certainly. But don't get me wrong. I think by now you know that I'm 110 percent in support of equality of the sexes, and I honor women above all else in this world. A woman with a goatee should make just as much money as a man with a goatee. Don't you agree? It's just hard for there to be any passion in a marriage when she's spent the day litigating a wrongful-death case and you've spent the day in the operating room. I don't think I'm off base here, do you? I hope you detect the fun and maybe a little exaggeration here; it is done to make a point.

When a man engages in roles that nurture his feminine side and his wife engages in roles that nurture her masculine side, what do you think is going to happen? In other words, if his feminine side is enhanced and his masculine side is diminished, and her masculine side is enhanced while her feminine side is diminished, what's the result? You can have a radical depolarization. You can have dramatically diminished attraction. You have essentially neutralized the very dynamic that attracted you together in the first place. It's not hard to see why so many couples today suffer from sexless marriages.

If this is you, you both need to regularly engage in activities that accentuate your sexual and polar differences. After all, desire is born from the "space" between you and your mate's polar differences. When those differences get blurred, polarity is lost and desire wanes. When you don't desire the one you are with, it's inherently tempting to look elsewhere for the experience of "desire."

Society's desire to homogenize the sexes drives me crazy. Waiters and waitresses have become servers. Stewards and stewardesses have become flight attendants. Why can't men and women be true to their natures? Our personal power comes from being true to ourselves; true to the essence of who we naturally are. Femininity does not equate to weakness nor does masculinity necessarily equate to insensitivity. A man shoveling snow off the driveway while his lady is baking apple pie isn't a demonstration of inequality; it's an exemplification of our polar differences.

What to Do?

So, what does this all mean in practical terms? What are you supposed to do to support the polarity in your marriage? Here are some ideas. Many of these overlap and could seem repetitive, but I expect one idea will resonate much more strongly with you than another.

1. **Honor and nurture your differences.** Your differences are what attracted you to each other in the beginning

and will help you maintain real attraction and polarity throughout your marriage. However, you must focus on the differences that attract you to her and defocus on the differences that make you want to hang yourself. The differences that figuratively make you want to cut your own throat were always there in the beginning; you just didn't notice them because you were "doped up" with chemicals that exist in your body to ensure the survival of the human race. You were seeing everything with rose-colored glasses. These special glasses are compliments of a sweet little love potion that your body produced when you were courting. This chemical elixir made up of scrotonin, oxytocin, and dopamine tends to wear off after about eighteen months, leaving you kind of spinning and wondering what the heck is happening? Her little habits, nuances, and perspectives on things now seem to bug the living crap out of you. This is your cue to immediately defocus on all the stuff that drives you crazy and start consciously focusing on what you love about your lady and worshipping those qualities. Honor her womanhood and femininity. Show her respect for who she is, and let her know through your words and actions that she doesn't have to change a thing to feel honored by you. Remember the short list of innate differences between the sexes from the previous pages. **Trust me, you don't want to change those.** You've got to let go, smile to yourself, and say, "You know, I'm really blessed to have a little crazy in my life." Put those rose-colored glasses back on and start seeing your woman as she really is—absolutely amazing and mystifying. All the trivial differences are just that, trivial.

2. **Stop trying to understand why she does what she does and thinks what she thinks.** You won't understand. It may be impossible to understand. But that doesn't make it wrong. It's just different from how you see it. Period! Letting go of the need to understand my wife was a huge turning point in my marriage. It eliminated destructive friction that usually manifested itself in heated arguments, the kind of arguments that once provoked my wife to want to jump out of a moving vehicle to get away from me. I'm talking about the kind of arguments that turn your bedroom into a walk-in freezer.

3. **Help your wife meet her basic human needs.** When you're the one responsible for her needs being met, you have instant HERO status. Women need a hero in their life and that hero should be you. She secretly wants a knight in shining armor as much as you want a princess. When her basic needs for security, food, shelter, and love aren't being met, it's difficult for her sensuality to reveal itself. When her needs for attention and significance aren't being met by you, her sensuality may ultimately be directed at whoever fills those needs for her. Yes, it goes both ways. Chapter 6 will talk in more depth about what your woman's needs are.

4. **Romance her.** A woman needs to be coaxed. She wants you to make her feel like a woman. She wants

and needs to feel desired. Bring her flowers. Call her at work. Leave her endearing notes. Arrange romantic outings. Treat her like a woman. Let her know you are thinking about her. Demonstrate that she is the most significant person in your life. Arrange a spa visit for her. Treat her like a woman worth pursuing and she will begin to respond like a woman worth pursuing.

5. **Act like a man.** This is huge because it is ultimately your manhood that coaxes her womanhood out of hiding. She wants a man who compels her to love and admire him. Take control of getting things done. Get that darn honey-do list done. Take a load off her plate. Give her some breathing room. Tell her you want her. Do innately masculine things that make her feel you are strong and capable of protecting and providing for her. Have a load of unsplit firewood delivered to the house and start splitting it with a big maul. Change the oil in your/her car yourself. Start working out if you don't already. If she suspiciously asks what's going on, tell her you decided you want to look good for her... because she deserves it!

6. **Allow her to be uniquely her.** To try and change her is to diminish her. Don't attempt to diminish the attributes that attracted you to her in the first place. If you diminish the differences, you diminish the polarity. If you diminish the polarity, sensual desire for each of you will evaporate. Letting go and allowing your woman to be herself is one of the greatest gifts you can give her. It will build or reestablish trust and help

to reignite her love for you. Embracing, honoring, and respecting her uniqueness with all her habits, quirks, and peculiarities by itself can take your relationship to new heights.

7. **Grow, man, grow!** Personal growth is a key element to having a fulfilling life and an outstanding marriage. As two people become more familiar with each other over time, the uncertainty and mystery that once fueled your desire for each other slowly diminishes. It is one of marriage's many paradoxes. The question is "How do you maintain a healthy sense of mystery and unfamiliarity while simultaneously growing emotionally more bonded?" The answer is in constant and never-ending personal growth and improvement. This means growing yourself as a human being so that the person you are tomorrow is an evolved version of who you are today. It means turning yourself into a book whose chapters are unfolding before your lover's eyes. It can be a bit unsettling to experience your mate or lover growing in complexity, but that is what keeps us on our toes. Personal growth doesn't necessarily have to be done alone, however. It can be a collaboration between you and your mate. You can pursue almost anything together with the understanding that you are each respectfully having your own experience with possibly different outcomes. Maintaining your individuality while simultaneously bonding with another is a balancing act, as is most anything worth pursuing.

8. **Be true to yourself.** Here is one of the great dichotomies and paradoxes of women. They want what they want, they want you to know what they want, and they want you to give them what they want. But sometimes what they really want isn't what they want at all but something much deeper than what they reveal on the surface. It's hard for me to write this without laughing out loud because this is what drives men out of their minds. Women are testing creatures. They are constantly testing your love, attraction, and commitment to them in often subtle ways. One of the unconscious ways they do this is by making requests and demands that test your manhood. What they are saying they want on the surface is not really what they want. What they want is to know that you are a man they can respect and trust and who is congruent. They want you to demonstrate that you will live true to your core, true to your calling, true to your higher purpose in life. Because that's what a man does, and she wants a real man in her life. That said, a real man will live his higher purpose and do it while meeting his wife's needs on a high level.

Home Sweet Home

When it comes to women, men have a built-in homing device. It's like a magnet being drawn to steel. Man came from woman, was introduced to the world through her vagina, and he spends the rest of his life trying to get back in. We also never seemed to have been completely weaned off the tit. Sounds like we're a bunch of big babies, right? Well, in my experience, most men never really do grow up. If they did, we might have a lot fewer wars and a lot more great marriages. Don't you think?

♥ Takeaways ♥

1. Men and women are not the same. In fact, we are polar opposites. This is what drives men crazy, but it is also the very thing that attracted us to women in the first place. We need to learn to embrace and appreciate these differences instead of trying to diminish them.

2. Support the polarity in your relationship by nurturing your natural masculine and feminine differences.

3. Be aware of how the blurring of masculine and feminine roles can diminish the polarity in your relationship. If your lady has a career that is traditionally masculine, she needs your support in nurturing her femininity when she is not at work. You may also need to support your sense of masculinity in ways that are new to you. It may also be worthwhile to evaluate your careers and home life and make sure they are in support of your relationship.

4. Take immediate steps to support the polarity in your relationship.

CHAPTER 5

GETTING ON
THE SAME PAGE

When a man spends his time giving his wife criticism and advice instead of compliments, he forgets that it was not his good judgment, but his charming manners, that won her heart.

—Helen Rowland

Indoctrination

Have you ever gone to a self-improvement seminar (without your spouse) like Tony Robbins's Unleash the Power Within? You come home totally juiced, ready to take your relationship, health, and business to a new level, fully expecting your partner to be as excited as you are. And then to your disappointment and confusion, she/he doesn't get it. They don't share your enthusiasm. You share, share, share, and share your new convictions, and they smile and say things like, "That's really nice dear" or "This is too much for me to handle all at once" or "What's this guy done to you?" Often they become intimidated and insecure because they don't feel like they know the "new and improved" you. Things may not have been very good before, but at least they knew what they were dealing with. This is a demonstration of the significance of beliefs and indoctrination in a relationship and how they can either bond you together or drive you apart.

One word that encompasses these concepts is religion. My definition of religion is any structured set of beliefs or concepts that influence your thinking and guide your decision making, which ultimately determines the quality of your life and your destiny. Indoctrination is the process of communicating these beliefs, concepts, and "doctrines" (religion) so that they become convictions. They become part of your updated "operating system," a new frame of reference by which your thoughts, actions, and decisions are modeled and tested. If you're consistently updating your operating system (through meditation, reading, attending seminars, pushing your personal boundaries, etc.) and your spouse is not, having a meaningful relationship can be challenging.

Beliefs are so powerful in determining your destiny that you have to consistently take stock of whether yours are holding you back or compelling you forward. Is your "religion" empowering you to have a better life? Hint: Any thought that you hold to be true is a belief. Any belief that causes you pain, limits the quality of your life, or prevents you from realizing your true potential needs to be seriously questioned and remodeled. The following would be examples of beliefs that might be firehosing your ability to get what you deserve in your relationship and in your life.

- Women are not as smart as men.
- Women should be subservient to men.
- I'm not smart enough to accomplish what I want.
- You have to have a college degree to get rich.
- You can't make money without taking it from someone else.
- Money isn't important.
- Money is the root of all evil.
- You have to work hard to make a lot of money.
- I can't have what I want because I'm short, fat, uneducated, ugly, a minority, one legged, blind, democratic, too old, from a dysfunctional family, computer illiterate, my daddy's in prison, etc.
- Sex is immoral.
- Sex is degrading.
- Kinky sex is dirty and therefore sinful.
- All men think about is sex.
- You can have a good marriage without sex.
- Men are always the high-desire partner.
- Women shouldn't initiate sex.
- All women want is…gee, I don't know.

- Women are impossible to please.
- Marriage is a ball and chain.
- Old dogs can't learn new tricks.
- I'm set in my ways.
- That's just who I am.
- I can't do it.
- I don't deserve the woman/man of my dreams.
- I don't deserve to have wealth.
- I'm not experienced enough to start my own business.

Okay, I think you get it. Here are a few poignant questions worth asking yourself to determine if you have beliefs that are sabotaging your life:

- Do your beliefs about yourself support your health and well-being?
- Do your beliefs about money support a financial well-being that takes the pressure off your wife/husband?
- Do your beliefs about God support a prosperous, inspiring, fruitful life full of joy, pleasure, meaning, and contribution?
- Does your belief about what is possible inspire you to pursue your dreams?
- Do your beliefs about women support and inspire you to a more fulfilling relationship? Do they make your wife feel worshipped?
- Do your beliefs about sex promote more sex or less sex? Do they inspire hot, wet, spiritual sex or cold disappointing sex?

- Do you have convictions about anything that cause emotional separation between you and your lover?
- Does your religious orientation cause friction between you and your mate?
- Does your obsession with anything make your mate want to jump off a cliff?

You can see now how significant your beliefs are at determining what comes into your life. Your beliefs are your guidance system that attracts to you what you have for good or bad. Do your beliefs support the kind of marriage experience that you want to have? Your beliefs are your autopilot, determining your destination by default. I highly recommend trashing any beliefs that sabotage your ability to experience a fruitful life and a passionate marriage. I don't care where they came from—your religion, parents, best friend, education, it doesn't matter. The Bible says, "By your fruits you shall know them." That's good enough for me.

Collaboration

So how in the heck do you get on the same page and stay on the same page with your spouse? You've got to collaborate on setting and accomplishing goals that you mutually benefit from. Collaborate on education and personal development. Collaboration in your marriage means sitting down and saying, "Hey baby, I know we've got a good marriage, but I want to take it up a notch. I want to be a better husband and learn to meet your needs better. I want our marriage to be the pinnacle experience in our lives. What do you say we go to this retreat I saw advertised?" It's agreeing to go to a "Baking for Couples" class to learn the art of making baguettes. Collaboration is choosing together to build your relationship toolbox.

If you can agree to work together on improving your health, adding exercise to your daily routine, enhancing your sex life, growing your communication skills, increasing the passion in your life, or taking your earning capacity up a notch, you move together in a common direction with similar indoctrination. It becomes easier to relate and have fun together, and you always have something to talk about. But most importantly, you are both growing as individuals and as a couple. Consistently spending quality time together where you are both enjoying and sharing experiences is one of the most collaborative things I can think of. Collaboration is collectively "choosing" your marriage and refusing to settle for mediocrity. It's working together towards a common end.

Riding a tandem bicycle is a powerful metaphor in action for collaboration in a relationship. You have two distinct positions on the bike, "captain" and "stoker." The captain is determined by nature, not debate or flipping a coin. The heaviest person goes in front (in the captain's seat) and is responsible for controlling the steering, braking, and avoiding obstacles. The stoker sits in the back and supports the efforts of the captain in terms of navigation, pedal power, and "bogey" spotting.

Tandem riders collaborate in that they are using the same mechanism to achieve similar goals. I say similar because as they both may want an exhilarating ride, their definitions of "an exhilarating ride" are usually quite different. He may want to push as hard as he can while she might want to sightsee a bit. His effort to ride faster pulls her along with him. Her desire to sightsee and share what she sees gives "Technicolor" to what otherwise might have been just a ride for him. The stoker's confidence and belief in the captain allows the stoker to let go and enjoy the ride. The captain's honor and respect for the stoker allows her influence as to what is a comfortable speed and desirable route.

Successful tandem riding is a perfect illustration of natural opposites unified as a complementary team. Much like dancing, there is a constant push and pull where the partners are never very far apart in the journey towards a common goal. **When you collaboratively meet each other's basic needs, marriage becomes the most extraordinary experience of your lifetime.** You'll be a great husband, have the wife of your dreams, and have an outstanding marriage.

I think having fun together is one of the most important spokes in the wheel of having a great marriage. Tandem riding fills multiple needs for me—quality time, fun, and staying fit together.

Tip 1: If your idea of personal growth is reading something like Squirms, Screams and Squirts: Going from Great Sex to Extraordinary Sex by Robert J. Rubel and expecting your wife to jump right in with you, think again. Remember the concepts of indoctrination and collaboration. She's got to be on the same page. If she's not, ease into it very slowly with tons of patience, zero expectations, and lots of love. I have a friend who is an avid sailor. It was a passion he wanted to share with his new wife, who was willing to give it a try but not without much trepidation. On her introductory sail, the weather began to turn for the worse. Instead of turning back to ensure that her maiden voyage was a good experience, as a "manly man" would do, he continued on to display his superior seamanship (stupidity). Rather than be impressed, she was terrified. Needless to say, she doesn't want to have anything to do with sailing ever again.

Tip 2: If you don't feel like you have the collaboration of your wife (or husband) in improving your marriage and sex life, all is not lost. Remember, none of this is about changing the other person. It's about changing yourself and becoming the person that the woman of your dreams wants. Usually, when you become the man of her dreams and treat her like she's the woman of yours, the relationship of your dreams will manifest itself.

🖤 Takeaways 🖤

1. Your beliefs and values determine the direction that you go in life. They regulate your perspective on things and ultimately your decision making. It's important that you and your mate have common values and beliefs so that as you grow, you grow together.

2. Collaborating on personal growth is a great way to grow together and fuel common interests within your marriage. That said, if you are truly growing as an

individual, you will more often than not pull up those around you as you inspire them through demonstration.

3. Collaborating on life is an experience of push and pull that takes a deep respect and honor of your inherent differences. It's allowing your mate to be who they are instead of who you think they should be. It's about respecting their role as your counterpart and celebrating your differences instead of letting them get under your skin. This ultimately fuels your polarity and in the long run attracts you to each other like a magnet to steel.

CHAPTER 6

THE SIX HUMAN NEEDS

One of the oldest human needs is having someone to wonder where you are when you don't come home at night.
— **Margaret Mead**

Dr. Gottman's "Love Lab"

Preeminent relationship psychologist and researcher Dr. John Gottman can predict with 91 percent accuracy which couples will get a divorce just by observing them arguing. In a lengthy study, randomly selected couples would spend the night in a mockup apartment that Dr. Gottman referred to as the "Love Lab." They agreed to communicate as naturally as possible while being filmed, recorded, and observed through one-way mirrors (unless of course they were in the bathroom or bedroom).

After years of research involving fifty couples, Dr. Gottman determined there are clues in an argument that signify a destructive path. These clues are: harsh startups, criticism, contempt, defensiveness, stonewalling, negative flooding, body language, failed repair attempts, and bad memories.

What's the significance of this to you? Well, if any of these things are going on in your arguments, you can forget about your woman wanting you and having any sex. Why? Because they are symptoms of a much deeper yet more fundamental problem that won't be solved by arguing or even more skillful arguing. Most therapists focus on enhancing communication skills and teaching people how to argue more effectively. Teaching people how to argue, however, is like selling them an antacid for indigestion. An antacid does not cure the root of the problem. It only helps mask the symptoms of the root of the problem. However, if you take care of the root of the problem, the symptoms go away on their own. So rather than teach you what not to do when in disagreement, I'm going to focus on what to do when everything is going okay.

What to Do!

In relationships, as in every other area of life, acting offensively is what moves you towards your objective. It's what scores you points in whatever game you're playing. Playing defense is never as fun or rewarding. Your probability of "scoring" is very, very low. When you have the ball—in other words, when you take responsibility for making a difference—you've empowered yourself. Remember, it's never about changing the other person. It's about changing yourself. It's about creating an environment that fosters love and passion in your relationship. It's about magnetizing yourself so that your partner wants you and wants to please you. It's about being the person that the woman or man of your dreams would be attracted to.

Setting the Stage

A passionate marriage doesn't just happen, especially within a monogamous relationship. When it does, the stage has always already been set for it. The stage or platform that all great marriages are built on involves maintaining a healthy level of polarity and reciprocally filling each other's needs. If you consistently do these two things, you will not only have a partner for life but, as life coach extraordinaire Tony Robbins once said, **"you'll have a love slave"** for life.

The Six Human Needs

Most problems in a marriage surface when one or more needs are not being met in the relationship. When exploring these six human needs, keep in mind that your lover might articulate their needs in different terms or may never have identified in words what they are. All humans have the same needs. They're just rarely ranked in the same order. Moreover, a woman's and man's needs are almost always in an inverse relationship to each other. This is one of the facts that makes understanding the opposite sex so difficult. You must grasp and embrace this concept if you want any chance of understanding your mate.

Mastery of this experience we call "relationship" is an ongoing, lifelong process, albeit the most rewarding. As you read through these six human needs, ask yourself: How can I meet these needs for my lover? Often the answers are very obvious, but sometimes not. As crazy as it sounds, most people don't really know what their lover wants and needs to feel fulfilled. Why? Maybe because you never asked! And maybe your mate never felt comfortable telling you because they thought you should know intuitively. And maybe your partner's needs are just not on your radar. It's time to turn your radar on or turn up its sensitivity. It will turn your marriage around on a dime.

Often, when you learn what your lover's needs are, the importance she places on them might not make any sense to you. It doesn't matter. Just respectfully embrace them and get to work being her man. Many of these things your mate needs you can offer as a supplier or source. Your contribution for most of them, excepting love, however, is acting as a conduit, facilitator, and supporter. Don't forget this is all about meeting the needs of your partner. You can't control your partner. You can't change your partner. You can't tell your partner what to do. But what you can do is inspire them. You can give them a whole new set of behaviors to respond to. You can create an environment that nurtures love, honor, passion, and respect. And I'm telling you, if you have love, honor, passion, and respect, you have the makings of a really hot and passionate affair with your mate.

As mentioned earlier, you might begin this process of discovery by asking your mate questions like "What can I do to make you feel more loved?" or "What, if anything, do you feel is missing in our marriage? I really want to know because you mean the world to me, and I want you to be happy." A more subtle (and genius) but more time-consuming way to identify which of your woman's needs might be deficient is to start taking your affection, listening skills, focus, and romance up a notch or two and see how she responds. If you are sensitive to her responses, you can often deduce what her deficits might be. That said, there is no substitute for just asking her what you can do to be a better husband and lover. What you deduce on your own may be at best only partially accurate and oftentimes completely off base. Thinking you can figure your woman out on your own without her offering some insights into the situation is folly. After all, she is a woman. This may seem to contradict a woman's desire for "a man who knows what she wants and takes pleasure in giving it to her," but sometimes we need to be thrown a bone. So let's get into the six human needs.

Human Need #1: Certainty/Security

We all need to have certainty in our lives. Certainty comes from many sources that are equally important, namely security, love, and health. Certainty is knowing that no matter what, your partner will be there for you and that you are unconditionally loved. Certainty comes from a belief in your resourcefulness, knowing that no matter what happens, together with your partner you can pull through anything. Security means not having to worry about putting food on the table or a roof over your head. It's knowing that the meeting of your physical needs is not in question. Certainty means not having to worry about the unknown. It enables you to sleep at night. Knowing that you are loved, cherished, and adored by your partner gives you certainty. Security also comes from believing in a higher power.

Guys: A woman feels certainty/security when she has no financial pressure. Don't ever allow her to be in a position where she feels financially insecure. For one, she deserves a life of certainty and comfort where she can be free to allow her femininity to flow, and two, it cuts off her desire for sex. When a woman feels honored and adored, she feels certain of her man's fidelity. When a woman's core values (namely security, love, and well-being) are not being met, it is difficult for her to fill secondary values such as sexual connection. She feels certainty knowing that you will give her the focused attention she needs to "talk through things."

Gals: A man may equally experience certainty in his strength (health), his ability to provide for his family, his belief in a higher power, and in your commitment to him. As revolutionary as this may seem, a guy finds certainty in having sex with his wife, whereas a woman generally wants certainty before having sex with her husband. For a guy, sex is a way of reconnection and reassurance that "everything is cool between us." It's also a good reset button for us at the end of a stressful day.

What provides each of us certainty may differ due to differences in gender and core values. Never assume that your partner's needs are the same as yours. You must walk in the direction of your partner in a spirit of reciprocity. Just because a guy doesn't feel like talking doesn't mean he shouldn't fill his woman's need to talk and do it lovingly. He will soon discover the reward in knowing and understanding his wife more intimately and will more willingly engage as time goes by. Likewise, just because a woman doesn't desire sex doesn't mean it's not at that moment an essential component to the health and well-being of their marriage and her husband's sanity. Curiously enough, the stereotypical roles described above can just as well be reversed.

Human Need #2: Uncertainty/Variety

In spite of our need for concrete certainty, life would be pretty boring without variety, surprise, and unexpected challenge. Hence our need for uncertainty. Too much uncertainty, however, breeds insecurity so there is a delicate balance to be maintained. For women, constructive uncertainty comes with never knowing what their lover may surprise them with next—a dozen roses, a romantic picnic under the stars, or perhaps an afternoon at the spa. For men, it comes naturally just being with a woman if she has embraced her femininity and is allowed to just be a woman. A woman's hormonal shifts, dramatic contrasts in perspective, and the dramatic unfolding of her mystery can be a fulfilling source of variety in a man's life.

Uncertainty also comes from taking on new challenges or learning new skills. It comes from journeying into new territory not always completely prepared. It's taking a road trip without any reservations. It's trying a new ethnic cuisine. It's adding a dash of spice to your life. It's taking your sexual experience to new levels. It's surprising each other! Never allow the fun and romance to become too predictable. Predictability breeds certainty, and too much certainty extinguishes the flame of desire.

Guys: Just a hint. Not knowing when you're going to be home is not the type of uncertainty a woman wants. Wondering if she's going to be able to make rent or not this month is not "healthy" uncertainty either. However, not knowing what romantic surprise you're going to spring on her is healthy uncertainty.

Guys: When I think of a man's desire/need for uncertainty, I think of the seven-year itch myth—a belief that boredom ensues from being with the same person over time. However, when women (and men) are encouraged to develop their skills, explore their desires, or pursue their passions, they're in a state of constant change and growth. I'm certainly not the same woman my husband married twenty-five years ago, and he is not the same man. If your spouse is not evolving, they may be stifled and in need of support from you to be true to themselves (their inner goddess.

Gals: A hint for you too. Not knowing whether it will be a week, a month, or a year before he has sex again is not "healthy" uncertainty. Never use sex as a bargaining chip or as leverage to get what you want. It is destructive to a relationship and demeans sex's value and meaning. However, not knowing what is coming next keeps him on his toes in a good way. Never be a foregone conclusion. Keep him guessing.

Gals: Sex is a basic human need. You wouldn't want to wake up and wonder "do I get to eat today?" Schedule biweekly sex to satisfy both of your needs; anything spontaneous is a bonus. Don't allow this to be a question mark for him.

Human Need #3: Significance

We all need to feel significant, that we are important to someone, and that our existence has meaning. We naturally seek ways to validate our uniqueness. We find significance in our careers, college degrees, achievements, societal roles, athletic prowess, size, strength, religious affiliations, the way we dress, and the clubs we belong to. We get significance in being a parent and a lover or provider. Some people meet this need through destructive means like alcohol, drugs, and criminal behavior. Within our marriage, we have a deep need to be significant to our spouse. That significance comes from consistent validation that we are the one they have chosen. We desire and need to know that we are appreciated—not once in a while but all the time. Everyone wants to know they matter and are not taken for granted.

Guys: She really wants to know that she's appreciated and that the second income she brings home (if this is the case) is a killer contribution. Yeah, I know you appreciate her, but she needs to know it daily. She needs to know that you appreciate her sharing her life with you. She needs appreciation for all the little things she does that make life easier for you. She needs appreciation for just being a woman. I personally have the highest reverence for women and exalt them above all else on earth. If she's a mother, she is by default one seriously significant human being. Let her know it.

Gals: A man gains much of his significance in life through providing for and pleasing his woman. Trust me on this. We feel like heroes every time we provide you any kind of pleasure, comfort, or solution to a problem. When you are happy, we feel like conquerors. If we buy a house you love, we feel significant. If we take you to a movie that you really enjoy, we feel responsible. If we take you out to dinner and you rave about how good it was, we feel like we cooked the meal ourselves. When you experience an orgasm, we feel extremely validated. If you are multiorgasmic, well, then we feel like gods.

Human Need #4: Love/Connection

Is love all you need? The answer is YES! And NO! No in the sense that love is just one of the six human needs. But yes in that if you love in the most complete sense of the word, your love will translate into the fulfillment of all six human needs. Most people in extended relationships say they love their spouse, but they don't really love their spouse. Mastery of love is not a destination but a journey, the journey of a lifetime.

What Love Is

There are three types of love; each is really important to understand in its relationship to marriage and sex: agape, philos, and eros.

Agape Love

Agape is Godlike love; it's unconditional and stretches across all humanity. It has no boundary and is in a spiritual sense divine. It's the love you have for mankind, the love that sends your heart out to starving children in Ethiopia.

Philos Love

Philos is friendship love. It's the meat and potatoes of a relationship. It fosters reciprocity, a give-and-take in the meeting of each other's needs. Philos is experienced between good friends, siblings, and spouses.

Eros Love

Eros is erotic love. It is the need for and expression of sexual desire, affection, and physical intimacy. Eros is the experience of falling in love. It's the feeling of euphoria when you are physically and emotionally attracted to your lover. It is romantic love.

What makes marriage so unique is that it is the only human relationship that encompasses all three kinds of love simultaneously. This is a powerful realization—and the reason why I believe that a great marriage is the pinnacle of human experience. I would be remiss not to include the following Bible text in a discussion on love. It describes what love is, I believe, in terms of agape and philos.

Love is patient, love is kind. It does not envy, it does not boast, it is not proud. It does not dishonor others, it is not self seeking, it is not easily angered, it keeps no record of wrongs. Love does not delight in evil but rejoices in the truth. It always protects, always trusts, always hopes, always perseveres. — *1 Corinthians 13:4-7 NIV*

Well, I think that about says it all. And since most of Western civilization is Christian, and most Christians have read or heard this very notable text, we should be a "nation of love" and love must be permeating our marriages and families. Right? Wrong! But why? Because most people are hypocrites. They're Sunday morning (part-time) Christians. I would love to go on an extensive rant about this, but it would digress too far from our subject. Maybe in another book. However, it is difficult to separate a discussion on love from spirituality and spirituality from religion. Let's suffice it to say that we need to move, with momentum, away from being part-time husbands and wives and start taking our roles seriously.

In fact, I'd like to suggest that you use the word "lover" in lieu of words like husband, wife, spouse, etc. You'll notice that I use it frequently in this book. It's a powerful demonstration of how vocabulary can change how you feel about something as well as its meaning. I use it because it alludes to eros love, and after all, this book is really about creating and nurturing desire in a marriage.

So how does one treat a "lover"? Lovingly, right? You treat them with affection; you frequently express your desire for them; you put them on a pedestal; you are endearing in your communications; you treat them like they are special. After all, the eros love that brought you together and will ultimately keep you together is what makes your relationship special from all others. Without eros, you are just friends, not lovers. Right? Is it easy to be impatient or unkind to a spouse, husband, or wife? Yes. How about a lover? No way! You don't dare say or do something hurtful to a lover. If you do, you're very quick to make amends and seek reconciliation. Why? Because we don't want to lose them. Why? Because they fill a need! Hmmm. Since when did your spouse, um... lover, cease to be your lover? Since when did we start taking our lover for granted? When we got married? No. When we had kids? No. When life got overwhelming? No. Your lover ceased being your lover when you stopped treating them like your lover!

This could be the most important distinction in this book so don't miss it. It's not enough to intellectualize this information; you've got to internalize it. Contrary to popular belief, knowledge is NOT power. Knowledge is "potential" power. The power comes in using the knowledge, in putting it into practice and making it a part of your operating system. It's taking the Sunday morning sermon to work with you. It's honoring your God, yourself, and your lover 24/7. It's acting with integrity and congruence. You can't completely love without integrity, and you can't really have integrity without love.

So let's turn the statement above into an affirmation you can take with you.

**"I will love my lover (husband, wife)
like a lover loves a lover."**

Love is the universal language that bridges all gaps and transcends all barriers. Love, if completely exemplified in a marriage, makes everything else in this book a moot point.

I'm reminded of the power in vocabulary. I recently introduced my husband to someone as my lover. It was fun to watch the surprise and confusion of our new acquaintance as he tried to ascertain what that meant and who this person was in my life. He was amused to later find out that my lover was also my husband.

Love is knowing your partner, for in knowledge there is strength. Couples who have an intimate knowledge of each other are better equipped to prevent and weather conflict and marital storms. What does it mean to know your partner? It means to be in touch. It means to always know what their desires, hopes, and dreams are. It means to know their beliefs, fears, and inhibitions. It comes from communicating about everything that is going on in each other's lives. It's knowing what makes them feel loved. How can you know someone if you don't know their rules for experiencing love?

Love is knowing what makes your partner tick, what juices them, what their passions are—and having the most current versions of these things. Love is communicating your needs to one another. It's knowing what her favorite flower, song, food, movie, and book is. Love is keeping the house stocked with White Zinfandel. Love is taking her dancing when you hate (I mean "prefer not to" sweetie) to dance. Love is never minding how long she takes to "get ready" to go anywhere. Love is you smiling every time you walk into your florally decorated bedroom. It is sharing the trivial as well as the significant.

Oftentimes when individuals look outside their marriage to have their needs for love met, it's because they've begun to live separate lives resulting from lack of knowledge of each other. We all remember "The Piña Colada Song" by Rupert Holmes. It poignantly exemplifies how often we look "outside" for what we already have near us. The song tells of a man who, bored with his relationship, looks in the personal ads for new possibilities. He finds an intriguing ad written by a seemingly very sensual woman looking for someone who likes Piña Coladas, getting caught in the rain, and making love on the beach. He responds to the ad and suggests meeting in a bar. Later, he waits in the bar for her only to see his "own lovely lady" walk in. He tells her that "he never knew" she likes Piña Coladas, etc., and that she was the lady he'd looked for. "Come with me and escape."

What Love Isn't

Here I will deviate from the track of only sharing positive "what to do's" and never any "what not to do's." There are a few behaviors I've commonly seen men direct towards their wives that I feel very strongly about because they're extremely immature, unloving, and a fast track to loss of connection and passion. I've been guilty of most of them at one time or another and have witnessed their potential destructiveness. The first of these things addresses what may actually be a seventh human need.

Possessiveness. One of the reasons we get married is to take our beloved off the market. We want to make them unavailable to anyone else and be at our disposal for the meeting of our personal needs. I know this is brash but true. Paradoxically, when we "take possession", we begin to erode one of the very things that attracted us to our mate in the beginning; and that is the energy and spirit that comes with a sense of personal freedom and autonomy.

What draws us to anyone is not their appearance but their energy. That energy is exemplified in their personal freedom of movement, of thought, and of expression. Their energy magnetizes and compels us to close the distance between us. However, if we close the distance too much, we lose our appreciation and awe for the object of our desire. Remember the concept of polarity in Chapter 4? This is another dualism in human psychology.

A person's need for love and connection is complemented by their need for freedom and autonomy. A caged bird will lose its love of life. Metaphorically, the door to the cage always needs to be open. It's all about respecting your mate enough to allow them their inherent right to choose their own course and be emotionally supported while doing so. It's about supporting them in being true to themselves and following their dreams whatever that means to them. Remember the moral to The Legend of Dame Ragnelle story? What a woman wants is the ability to choose her own course. Don't we all want that?

Criticizing her. When Cupid's love potion has worn off, we often feel too comfortable in expressing our "true" feelings about the little things (i.e., petty minutia) that we don't like about our mate and that we would like them to change. This often manifests itself as harsh censure but can also be disguised as "loving, well-intentioned criticism." No matter how you communicate it or how well-intentioned it is, criticism has no productive place in a marriage. It erodes trust, intimacy, and desire. It's impossible for your mate to "want you" as her man when you demean her and make her feel bad. There is no love in criticism. Not in a marriage.

In our society, most women are very self-conscientious of their physical appearance. From a young age, we are bombarded by the media's false standards of how a woman should look. We compare ourselves to magazine cover models who are unusually gifted and often airbrushed. Making any comments to your lady about her physical appearance that can even be construed as negative can make her uncomfortable baring her body to you. If her nakedness and the activities that often go along with it is something you yearn for, focus on only the positive and keep all other thoughts to yourself. Just remember, the pin up models aren't the ones sleeping with you—your wife is!

Interrupting her while she's talking. It means you're not listening. It means you're not respecting her. It means you are self-absorbed. It means, in that moment, she's not being loved. I thank my wife for consistently and lovingly pointing this behavior out to me. It was always a shock because I didn't know I was doing it until she said something.

Talking over her as if what you have to say is more important. It means you're not really listening. It means you're not respecting and honoring her. It diminishes her significance and says that you hold yourself in higher regard than her.

Correcting her behavior, especially in front of other people. I thank my Uncle Phil for pointing this out to me twenty-five years ago when I was a newlywed. He said, "If you keep that up, you're going to lose her." It was a huge blow to my ego, for I thought I was "making her a better person." What a jerk I was!

Censoring what she says to other people because you're concerned about what they'll think of you. Again, how self-centered of you and demeaning to her. It doesn't matter whether she tells the story correctly or gets facts mixed up. It doesn't matter if she's breaking your rules for social interaction. They're your rules not hers, and it's not your job, place, or right to censor her. Love means embracing an individual for who they are and letting go of the differences. Always focus on what you love and admire, never on what you don't.

Making condescending comments. This is nothing but a crude maneuver to stroke your own ego by tearing someone else down. We can do this in the most cutting ways or sometimes in the smallest joking ways. Ever make a comment or joke designed to diminish your loved one's stature, intelligence, or significance and then say, "I didn't mean anything by it" or "It was just a joke"?

Needing to get the last jab. During a fight, have you ever said something hurtful that was responded to with something more hurtful? Don't get into that death spiral, and don't be the one who has to get in the last jab. We can always say something more hurtful than she can. We're guys. We can string more base profanity together in one sentence than a woman will usually use in a lifetime. Don't let this hurtful, perverse behavior into your arguments or fights.

Focusing on meeting your own needs. Love means seeking to meet the needs of your mate without expecting anything in return. Ultimately, meeting each other's needs becomes a symbiotic dance of exchanging leads. A great marriage becomes the perfect demonstration of perpetual reciprocity.

Human Need #5: Growth

Marriage is the ultimate opportunity for growth. And growth equals expansion. Expansion means living more, loving more, and everything that implies. It implies that you expand emotionally, mentally, physically, financially, spiritually, and sexually. Someone once said that you're either growing or dying. Think about it; nothing can live in a stagnant pond. It's dead, devoid of life.

Growth is a fundamental human need because it is the process of moving forward to self-realization and knowing God, whatever God means to you. Growth is what makes you feel alive.

Interestingly enough, growth does not come naturally to many people, and marriage offers you the biggest opportunity for it. Problems in a relationship are a blessing in disguise. They are a signal that something needs to change, that it's time to grow. If you have a health problem, you take it head-on and make radical changes in your lifestyle. A health problem is a wake-up call that you have been doing one or many cumulative things wrong. If you have a problem in your business, you tackle it, learn from it, make whatever changes are required, and grow the business to the next level. In business, whenever you have a problem you don't say, "That's just the way I am."

If you think about it, no one can really be happy doing the same thing at the same level for very long. You will either get bored and frustrated or you will push yourself to new levels that keep you challenged. You either grow or you die. We grow by learning new skills and languages, by taking on new challenges, by stretching outside our comfort zone. We grow by entertaining new paradigms, by considering the needs of others before our own. Growth always provides perspective because you can only appreciate where you are by looking back at where you've come from.

Contributing to an environment that allows your partner to grow is a mature act of love. Examples of this might be providing for and supporting her in:

- tennis lessons
- art classes
- foreign language classes
- specialty cooking classes
- starting a new business
- a spiritual retreat
- a couples' Kama Sutra retreat
- a horsemanship clinic
- reading a book together on How to Have an Outstanding Marriage
- learning to ride a motorcycle or fly an airplane
- taking her to dance lessons

Growth Is, Well...Growing Up!

Growth is also a huge part of maintaining the polarity and consequently the dynamic of desire in a marriage. When your partner is growing, learning, changing, and evolving, it keeps you on your toes. It helps you maintain a sense of wonder, interest, and curiosity in them. Growth helps support the differentiation between two people that is necessary for sensual desire.

I enjoy privately starting a new hobby to surprise my husband with proficiency at something unexpected or slightly out of character. Years ago, I decided I wanted to start playing tennis. I coaxed my husband into a first try at it while on vacation. After thirty minutes of James chasing my errant balls, he finally threw his back out in a gallant effort to hit a wayward shot. I subsequently spent the next few months secretly taking tennis lessons so that I could surprise him with a competitive game on our next vacation.

It's important to do the happily unexpected. In doing so, you become an unfolding mystery that breeds healthy uncertainty.

Human Need #6: Contribution

Contribution is your way of giving back, of making a difference. It's your participation in making the world a better place. It's not uncommon for people to struggle with having a sense of purpose in their lives. "Why am I here?" or "What's the point of my life?" are questions that eventually come up once the noise and glitz of modern life start to fade in significance. We need to feel that our lives "have meaning" as Viktor Frankl put it in his monumental book Man's Search for Meaning. The answer to the "meaning" question is almost always found in tandem with the answer to the "contribution" question and in the filling of our need for significance.

Every person has a unique talent, gift, or insight. Our unique gift might be our intense passion for something that people aren't normally passionate about. It might be cooking, tennis, gardening, mechanical engineering, teaching, voice, guitar, sculpting, medicine, massage, writing, hairstyling, shrub trimming, inventing, speaking, or the gift of prophecy. Whatever your gift, talent, or passion, the one thing you need to appreciate most is that we each have a unique way of expressing that gift, talent, or passion. We each have a unique "voice." That's why every art form in the world never runs out of individuals to express its interpretations. Every painter, singer, sculptor, composer, graphic designer, cake decorator, and jeweler is unique. Likewise, every physician, dentist, engineer, carpenter, teacher, mother, and yoga instructor is unique. We may not be in a unique line of work, but we certainly have a unique way of communicating our work and expressing it to the world.

So how can we each best serve our fellow man and contribute most significantly? This is my answer to the question. In your marriage, support each other's need to contribute whether that means putting twenty bucks in the plate at church, donating to a local charity, or being an outstanding parent. Your greatest contribution might come in raising children in a non-dysfunctional environment. I can't think of one more significant or honorable. Maybe your contribution is being the best husband or wife you can be to set a higher standard for friends and family. I am certain the biggest contribution you can make to society at large is in your own home.

Nevertheless, I think that life's true purpose is to be true to yourself. When you dig deep and find that thing that stirs your passions and lifts you to a higher place—that love for something that must be shared in a way only you can share—you'll find that part of yourself. Being true to yourself is living your "personal legend" as Paulo Coelho explains in his book The Alchemist. It's living your passion and expressing it in the way that only you can, using your unique "voice." And in the process, your scent, your flavor, your essence will linger and the world will be a better place because of you.

♥ Takeaways ♥

1. Create an environment that sets the stage for love and passion in your relationship.

2. Be the person that the woman or man of your dreams would be attracted to.

3. Help support and fill your mate's six human needs for:
   a. certainty/security
   b. uncertainty/variety
   c. significance
   d. love
   e. personal growth
   f. contribution

4. Above all, "Love your lover the way a lover loves a lover."

CHAPTER 7

YOUR GAME FACE
(How to "Bring It" Every Day)

"Your state of mind is the most important factor in the outcome of your life."
—Ziad K. Abdelnour

E verything I've shared so far will do you no good if you are not consistently in a state of mind to put it into practice. One of the single most powerful concepts to master in your life is the ability to control your "state." By state, I'm referring to your state of mind. What the heck does this have to do with your relationships or creating passion and desire? Everything! Your mental state equals the state of your relationship. The caliber of your thinking, or the psychology that you consistently bring to your interactions with your mate, determines the quality of your relationship. And ultimately, the quality of your relationship equals the quality of your life.

You have the ability to massively influence your circumstances whether you know it or not. And you can exert this influence solely through your state. I'm not talking about the Power of Positive Thinking here, although that's part of it. What I'm talking about is learning to put yourself into an empowered frame of mind so that your circumstances bend to your will.

We've all experienced times when everything just seemed to go right. You know, when you felt like you were at the top of your game. You were 280 ft. off the tee and setting up for an eagle. You just knew it was there. You had the "feel." No pressure, just a Zen-like confidence. You were in the flow. Have you ever had an experience when you felt like you were performing your best at work? You got up that morning, went for a five-mile run, had a healthy breakfast, kissed your wife good-bye, and drove to work expecting to really take it up a notch. You felt like you could take on anything and finally reel in that big account for the company.

In sports, particularly those requiring individual efforts like golf and tennis, the power of "state" is clearly exemplified. Top golfers like Jordan Spieth, Jason Day, and Rory McIlroy consistently place in the top ten of the tournaments they play. Why? Not because they are mechanically better golfers but because they consistently show up in a state that empowers them to play their best under pressure. Tiger Woods won as often as he did because he showed up consistently in a superior state. He was like, "I play in a league of my own. I'm not even going to acknowledge the presence of these other guys." Since Tiger's divorce scandal, he hasn't been able to regain the state that made him so great on the golf course.

Are Federer, Djokovic, and Nadal all mechanically better tennis players than Ferrer, Wawrinka, and Tsonga? Not necessarily. Then why have they dominated the top three rankings for years? Because they always show up expecting to win and don't allow the "problems" they face in their matches to affect their performance. They always "bring it." And likewise, you've got to always "bring it" to your marriage. Being in a positive, resourceful state is likened to having your A-game turned on. State is everything! The quality of your state equals the quality of your relationship.

So how does this specifically apply to your marriage? Well, for starters, if your state is high and hers is high, the quality of your relationship will be high. If you both have low states, the quality of your experience will be low. If your state is high and hers is low, your job is to throw her a "lifesaver" and raise her state to a higher level and so on. Whatever you expect in your relationship, you will look for evidence to support. Whatever you expect from your mate, you will look for evidence to support your expectations. In other words, if you think your mate is a bitch and approach the day thinking I wonder what bitchy thing she's going to say today, all you're going to see is anything that you can construe as bitchiness.

Ever looked for something in the fridge you remembered as red but it was really yellow? You can't find it even though it's right in front of your face. We see what we expect to see. We find what we are looking for. We manifest what we expect. If our state is strong enough, we will bring those around us up to our level or down to it as the case may be. Our state determines what we expect. If we are optimistic, we look for the good in everything. And what will we find? The good! If you want the wife of your dreams, then act like she is the woman of your dreams, expecting the results you want.

How to Access a Quality State at Will

Personal development coach Tony Robbins teaches the importance of learning to master your state, and I thank him for introducing me to the concept many years ago. Your state is determined by three primary things. I have personally tested and proven these things to be responsible for any state you experience, barring those induced by drugs or medical conditions outside your control.

The Three Components of State Are...

Physiology

Physiology is the study of the relationship of all your bodily systems to one another. In this context, we could call it your physical self. What you do with your body directly affects how you feel. Your posture, movement or lack thereof, facial expressions, and depth of breath all affect how you feel. Did you know that it's almost impossible to feel depressed when you have good posture, breathe deeply, and move around quickly with a smile on your face? Try it next time you feel low. You'll pick yourself right up. If you look closely at anyone who's depressed, what do you see? You see slumped shoulders, shallow breathing, and dragging feet.

Notice your own physiology when you feel on top of the world. You see that you have good posture, your head is held up high, and you move around with intention. Tennis is my favorite sport to illustrate the relationship between emotional state and physiology. I saw a match between Americans James Blake and Andy Roddick. I think it was the third set with Blake down two sets and starting to lose ground in the third. You could see his attitude deteriorating along with his physiology. His shoulders had dropped, his face looked defeated, and he started walking more slowly. You could see him beating himself up, and the more he beat up on himself, the worse he played. Then something really cool happened. The crowd got behind him and started cheering him on. The crowd's energy lifted his spirits, broke his disempowering state, and inspired him to play his all-out best. He turned the game around, won the third set, and kept the match going. I think he eventually lost but did it with dignity.

Learn to assess your physiology and make adjustments on the spot.

Another significant aspect of physiology is your general state of health. If you're not healthy, it's hard to feel good. If you don't feel good, it's hard to be in a good state. If you're overweight, you can't move with spring in your step. If you don't get enough sleep, you'll be dragging your tail around. If you don't take care of yourself physically with a good healthy diet and exercise routine, how can you put your A-game on? You owe it to yourself and your family to be the best YOU that you can be.

The best way for me to change my physiology is with exercise. It gives me energy and often acts as a reset button giving me space to remember what's most important in my life. It's also an opportunity to put stressful situations into perspective; that all things only have the meaning we give them, good or bad. Even though your thoughts dictate your actions; your actions can change your mood and how you're feeling at any given time. I've noticed for example that by acting sexy, it makes me feel sexy.

Focus

Whatever we focus on seems to manifest in our lives. Whatever we give attention to grows and becomes a dominant part of our experience. Your focus is what you are concentrating on with your physical eyes and your mind's eye. It's what you think about consistently. If you focus on what's beautiful about your mate, that's what you will see and respond to. If you focus on the habits and idiosyncrasies of your mate, they will dominate your perception of that person. Focusing on what you have control over in your life empowers you to make a difference. Focusing on what is outside your control, like your partner's bad habits, will drive you crazy, make you reactionary, and bring out the jerk in you. When you look for the good in a situation, you'll find it. If you look for what stinks, you'll always find something that stinks even if you have to subconsciously manufacture it. This breeds frustration, anger, and resentment.

If you think about what is beautiful in your life and everything you have to be thankful for, you'll experience the emotion of gratitude. Gratitude sure feels better than resentment. Always remember that an attitude of gratitude raises your altitude. In fact, it's difficult to experience any negative emotions when you are in a state of gratitude. Something to be grateful for, don't you think?

For as he thinketh in his heart, so is he.
— **Proverbs 23:7**

Another powerful type of focus is experienced through prayer and meditation. Stay tuned. I don't want to lose you on this one because it is really fascinating. A contemporary way of describing the power of prayer and meditation is in using the words "focused intention." You've probably at least heard of the book The Secret by Rhonda Byrne. The underlying message in The Secret is that you will manifest in your life whatever you focus on with congruence. In other words, when you align your focus, your thoughts, your intentions, and your actions to the same outcome or desire, the pieces to your puzzle seem to fall together effortlessly. I don't know about the "effortlessly" part, but I can tell you with certainty that when your focus, intention, and actions are all in alignment, your congruence attracts the object of your intention into your life.

Praying for yourself or others has always been a faith-based practice with an efficacy largely unexplainable. Recent research has shown that not only can prayer and intention significantly affect your own health, well-being, and behavior but also that of others. Participants in a study in Hawaii were all hooked up to functional magnetic resonance imaging (fMRI) in an isolated environment. On a schedule unknown to the participant, spiritual healers would send prayers and focused intention for the well-being of the participant. According to the scans, at precisely the same times that the participants were being prayed for or focused on with positive intention, certain areas of their brains would activate.

The only insight I want you to take from this is the possibility that your mate is influenced by your feelings, your thoughts, and your intentions whether you are in their presence or not. Being in an empowered and loving state towards your wife is imperative even when you're not with her. She will subconsciously pick up on it, and it will predispose her feelings and behavior towards you before you even have a chance to get your foot in the door. The message?

Deeply focus on your lady for moments throughout the day. Send her love as if in a prayer. Not only will this help set her emotional stage for a more loving reception, but it will also help you maintain a lovingly empowered state. Think of it as a pre-shot routine.

>>>—♥—→

The juiciest part of life is found in the present when I'm focused on the positive in my mate, my daughter... my life.

It's so true that yesterday is history, tomorrow is a mystery, and today is all you really have. Be mindful not to drag baggage from the past into the present. Always expect the best from your mate. Don't treat them like a stagnant individual resistant to change, even if that's what you're used to. Always act with the expectation that they will respond to you with a new empowering behavior.

I'm disappointed when someone treats me like the Kimberly I once was and not the new and improved model that awakened this morning.

The Power of Questions

The questions we ask ourselves can determine our focus. Thinking is not much more than the internal process of asking and answering questions. Here are examples of benign questions that probably won't impact your state one way or the other:

- Should I take a shower?
- What should I wear?
- This belt or that?
- Breakfast at home or on the run?
- I wonder what's for dinner?
- I wonder when Daylight Saving Time starts?
- I wonder if we're going to have sex tonight? (On second thought, if you have to wonder this too often, your state will probably deteriorate as a result.)

Here are examples of disempowering questions that will negatively affect your state. These questions predispose you to negativity and un-resourcefulness. Negative questions yield negative answers. If you're looking for answers in your life, you certainly don't want the answers to the following questions showing up. Whatever you focus on seems to show up consistently whether you like it or not. Be careful of questions like these:

- Is my boss going to pressure me today?
- Is my wife going to be the usual nag she always is?
- When should I start a diet?
- Why does this always happen to me?
- Why is it always someone else getting the raise?
- Why don't I ever win the lottery?
- What's my wife's problem?
- Why do my kids hate me?
- Why don't I have enough money?

- Why did that jerk cut me off?
- I wonder if I'm going to hit it in the water like always?

These questions put your mind in the gutter because if you look for thistles, you will find thistles. If you look for roses, you'll find roses. Your choice. Now let's take a look at some empowering questions. By empowering, I mean questions that elevate your thinking. Questions that result in answers that provide tools to get what you want. Questions that tap into your resourcefulness. Questions that make you feel good just by asking them. Questions like:

- How did I get so blessed to have you in my life?
- What can I do today to make my wife feel more loved?
- What is within my power to make a difference in the environment?
- What three things could I do today to boost the quality of my marriage?
- What could I do to double my income in the next year?
- How can I capitalize on my unique skills to make some extra money?
- What unique opportunities are there in this recession?
- What one thing could I do today to move closer to my fitness goals?
- What do I love most about my children?

- What are three things I'd like to change in my life, and what single step can I take today towards that change?
- If I could make my living doing anything I wanted, what would it be?

Notice how these questions affect your physiology just reading them. Do you feel yourself breathing deeper, maybe holding your head higher? How about your face? Does it feel a little more relaxed? Isn't this the way to think? Can you see the track we're on here? Never focus on what you don't want in your life. Focus only on what you want. On the goal. On the ideal. Never even acknowledge the water you have to hit over to reach the green. Focus only on the pin and oh how big the green is you're hitting to. Focus only on what you are grateful for in your life and on new possibilities. Slip on some metaphorical rose-colored glasses and remember what you love about your woman. Now that's what I'm talking about!

Language

The last component of building an empowering state is the language you use both internally and externally. By language, I mean how you express yourself, the vocabulary you use. The way you describe things becomes your reality of those things. For me, this is very powerful because it demonstrates another area of control that I have over my reality. The only truth your brain knows and responds to is what you tell it. If you got a flat tire on the way home and you describe your day as being "ruined," how are you going to feel? What kind of state are you bringing home to your family? How different would it feel if you described the experience as "interesting" or "enlightening," as in "Gee, I didn't know how hard it was to get the spare tire out from underneath the car!" or "Good thing that happened to me and not my wife. I better do a how to change a tire workshop at home so she can handle it if it ever happens to her."

When someone cuts you off in traffic, how do you respond? Do you say, "Wow, that was close," or do you say, "What a jerk," and flip them the bird? Can you guess which statement leaves you in a more pleasant state? If the last thing you said to someone was "What a jerk," how do you think your first interaction with the next person in line will be? If you say to yourself that you "never" have sex anymore, whether true or not, "never" will become a self-fulfilling prophecy. Do you have "devastating" experiences in your life on a daily basis? Or is life "great" no matter what happens?

When I was a kid, my grandfather "Pappy" lovingly reprimanded me when someone asked me how I was and I answered something like, "Fine, thank you." He would say, "When someone asks you how you are, you tell them that you are GREAT! And you say it with emphasis." I now know how wise he was. It always put me in a better state and made me feel bigger than I really was. What kind of a "pantywaist" response is "fine" or "okay"? Here's a list of words you might consider incorporating into your communications with yourself and others. They make you feel good just saying them.

Awesome—Delicious—Super—Wealth
Great—Dynamic—Abundance—Sexy
Perfect—Exceptional—Breakthrough—Nutritious
Amazing—Solutions—Brilliant—Magic
Beautiful—Outstanding—Epiphany—Fascinating

Now here's a list of example words to avoid using. They can get you feeling depressed, or at least disempowered, in a heartbeat.

Can't—Devastating—Hopeless—Lousy
Won't—Ruined—Bitch—Sick
Should—Afraid—Disaster—Okay
Could—No—Terrible—Stressed
Hate—Suffer—Failure—Worried

These words suck! Don't allow them into your thoughts or conversations. Get in the habit of censoring your thoughts and words. There are alternative ways to describe your thoughts and experiences that are more empowering. Like my Pappy used to say, "If you can't say something positive, don't say anything at all."

It's hard to have your A-game on when you are overcommitted and overextended. It's important to make decisions that serve you and your family's well-being. Before you take on another project that could significantly impact an important facet of your life, give yourself a reality check by first asking yourself how that decision will affect your health and well-being and ultimately that of your family.

I think the ultimate barometer is to ask yourself "Will I still be emotionally, mentally, and physically available to my mate as they deserve?" Another poignant question is "Will this negatively affect the quality and/or frequency of our love making?"

♥ Takeaways ♥

1. When you learn to bring a quality, resourceful, playful state to your relationship, those things that you have perceived as problems will often evaporate or transform into opportunities for you to grow and be a better mate. When you are in an empowered state of mind, you change how you act and react to your environment. You change how your environment reacts to you. When you are in an empowered state, mountains are reduced to molehills and the trivialities that used to irritate you vanish. When you are in a quality state of mind, you become someone who others want to be around and associate with because your presence makes them feel good.

2. Mastery of "state" is essential in consistently applying the principles in this book.

3. The quality of your questions and language equals the quality of your thinking. The quality of your thinking

and physiology equals the quality of your state. The quality of your state equals the quality of your relationship and of your life. So always think:

What am I doing with my body?

What am I doing with my mind?

What am I doing with my language?

These three things determine your state for good or bad, and you have the power to influence them NOW. So do it! Bring your A-game to the table now and always. You owe it to yourself. You owe it to your wife!

CHAPTER 8

BACK FROM THE EDGE

Some people claim that there's a woman to blame, but I know, it's my own damn fault.

—**Jimmy Buffet**, "Margaritaville "

Don't Be a Statistic

If your marriage is devoid of a healthy and satisfying sex life, you might just be asleep at the wheel and in need of a wake-up call. I recently read that, including first, second, and third marriages, 67 percent of marriages end in divorce. Let's just assume for conversation's sake that 67 percent is the real number and that two out of three marriages are history. Assuming the number is correct, here's my question: is there a direct correlation between the current divorce rate and the percentage of people experiencing problems with sex in their marriage? Check this out!

In 2006, NBC's Dateline surveyed 27,500 people over four days. Out of all who participated, 22 percent said that "sex was alive and well" in their marriage and 10 percent said it was "robust, erotic, and passionate." However, 33 percent said their sex life was "asleep and needing a wake-up call," 22 percent said it was "comatose and in danger of dying," and 13 percent said "sex life is dead." Notice the coincidence? All told, 68 percent of the couples expressed problems with sex or sexual desire, and the divorce rate is around 67 percent. You think there might be a direct correlation between the two? I know there is.

The question now is are people getting divorced because they're not having sex, or are they not having sex because their marriage is not healthy or "on the rocks"? The answer is both. Sex results from intimacy in a relationship, and it promotes and nurtures intimacy in a relationship. Meaning, you generally won't have sex without a great marriage, and you won't have a great marriage without sex. That's why sex should never be used as leverage to get what one wants in a relationship. If sex is withdrawn, intimacy and connection are lost. Then you're back to the chicken or the egg. What are you supposed to have first? Intimacy or sex? Well, again, the answer is both. And that's why it's imperative that couples work together to meet each other's needs—her need for intimacy leading to sex and his need for sex to provide intimacy.

Is this the perfect conundrum? Maybe. But as I say in other chapters, don't fight it. Don't fight Mother Nature. Embrace her and your world will magically transform into a better place! When a man works to meet his woman's need for intimacy and she works to meet her man's need for sex (or vice versa), a new language is formed between you that makes sex happen more spontaneously. That language is the language of love.

Is This YOU?

I don't think a month goes by that I don't make a new acquaintance that's getting a divorce. The funny thing is that the men consistently don't see it coming. They wake up with the ominous note on the pillow saying something like, "I can't take anymore. I'm leaving you. Have a nice life."

Additionally, I know people who are divorced in spirit yet remain married for convenience. Let's face it. Divorce is expensive, not to mention one of the most stressful experiences a person can have.

On a recent flight to New York I sat next to a man we'll call Doug. While exchanging pleasantries, he asked what I "do." I told him that I am a marriage coach and educator and have studied happily married couples that have been married for at least twenty years. He responded that he qualified for the "at least twenty years" part but was not so sure about the "happily married" part. He said he had been married for forty-five years and that most of his friends and siblings were still married to the same person after thirty-five plus years. I thought I had hit the jackpot and might come away with a bundle of valuable insights.

That I did, but not what I expected. As far as he knew, no one in his circle of friends was really happy in their marriages including him. He was convinced that "the expectation people have of a glorious, passionate marriage is unrealistic." He and his wife really didn't enjoy being together, they had different interests that they never shared, and he never seemed to be able to give her what she wanted because she would never tell him what that was until he was in trouble for not doing it. He hinted that they did not have sex and clearly had no "marriage." Yet they seemed to have no intentions of getting a divorce, at least none that he knew of. I thought this was interesting so I dug deeper.

Doug explained that most of his lifelong friends and siblings who were married for thirty-five or more years went to the same Midwestern schools, belonged to the same Midwestern church, and remained in the same Midwestern town their whole lives. He further explained that "settling" for the "reality" of marriage was what he and his friends did. Wow! I thought. Why would all these "lifers" settle for such an uninspiring, mediocre experience? And then the picture began to unfold. What was the mire holding these couples together? Small communities? Religious indoctrination? Social pressure? Poor examples of "normal"? Lowered expectations? Fear of change?

The answer was all of it. I thought, *Oh my God! This is the first of the baby boom generation, and if this isolated group of people is at all reflective of this demographic, how many people are really happily married? Something's got to be done about this. If this group is that screwed up, their parents must have been equally poor at marriage, and their children are probably following their example. These people have limited, if any, marriage skills! They are clueless. We need to get some help out there.*

This sentiment was reinforced when Kimberly and I encountered a couple while out for an evening stroll. They appeared to be in their late fifties or early sixties, and you could just tell they had been together a long time. We eagerly engaged them, excited to find out how long they had been married and what their secret to a great marriage was. We were both shocked to find out that a "great marriage" was not part of their experience and that their secret to staying together was "to have low expectations." Low expectations? You've got to be kidding me! Low expectations are the secret ingredient for mediocrity, not greatness. The scary part was that they were both psychologists and both highly published authors. That's when I became determined to develop training and coaching programs where we teach couples how to turn the relationship they have into the most fulfilling part of their lives.

My wife and I were visiting with a friend I had known for twenty-five years or so. She had been married all those years and had four children ages fifteen, ten, eight, and five. Kimberly and I observed over two days that Emily and her husband, Tim, (names changed for privacy) rarely if ever made eye contact and never talked to each other, except short directives regarding the kids. It was obvious they had no "marriage" but rather had built a "company" for the rearing of children. I felt sadness and concern and looked for a way to engage Emily. Knowing how crazy our life is with one child, I asked if they had a date night every week to ensure emotional and physical intimacy between them. Her response was very alarming. She said, "We used to, but not really anymore. It's gotten harder as the kids have gotten older and involved in more activities. There's always something going on every night of the week, and the kids take priority."

I read that as a death knell for their relationship, and it showed in their interaction, or lack thereof, with each other. No emotional intimacy, no sex. I also saw the crazy family schedule as a smokescreen that covered the absence of any real connection between Emily and Tim.

The three preceding stories are not anomalies. They represent the gross majority of relationships that I've come across in my research. "Bogey" and "Double Bogey" have become scores that too many people are settling for. Don't settle!

No Intimacy and Sex?

For now just forget about the sex for a while. You need to take care of the main thing, your connection with your lover—which means study this book and use the information to create an environment where love and passion grow and thrive. When there is no sex happening in the relationship, all I can say is watch out! You may very well have a loving "solid" relationship that just needs some TLC; applying the principles in this book will get you back on track and bring intimacy, desire, and sex back into your marriage. However, if she has overtly communicated that she's just not interested in you anymore sexually or she's just not interested in you at all, you've got work to do and you need to do it fast. You've got to make some dramatic changes. You've got to dig deep and get her attention.

If this is where you are, you need to work in earnest to gain her trust back, build polarity between you, and start making her feel wanted and desired. She needs to feel your focus, attention, and love like never before. And you need to start right this minute. You don't have tomorrow. You don't know where her threshold of pain is. She could be teetering on the precipice of looking for love somewhere else. She needs you to man up and go after her right now.

Here are some ideas to get your mind working. They are to the point and you can expand on them yourself.

1. Tell her you've been a jerk and have not been a good husband and that you just read this really cool book on how to be a great husband, and you want to spend the rest of your life loving her, honoring her, respecting her, supporting her dreams, treating her like the queen she is, and meeting all her needs.

2. Find out (from her) which of her needs aren't being met, and start filling them on her terms!

3. If you are overweight, cut the unhealthy carbs and get your ass on an exercise program. NOW!

4. If you've always had a mustache or beard, shave it. If you don't, grow a tasteful goatee. The point is that you need to shake things up a bit and get her attention back. If you happen to know that she loves the way you already look, you can ignore this suggestion.

5. Start wearing fresh, new, different clothes.

6. Send her flowers and chocolates.

7. Romance her as you did in the beginning. If you weren't a romantic, stretch yourself a bit and do something out of character. Maybe she's bored with you. Make

arrangements to take her to that one activity you always avoided, and make a big production out of it.

8. Never criticize her, argue with her, or demean her in any way.

You have to change her association with you, which is probably negative. If your marriage is falling apart and/or dispassionate, she may likely feel bad every time you walk into the room and vice versa. You must begin to give her a positive association to you and you must do it now. If you haven't waited too long, any glimmer of change can give her hope.

I'd suggest a little subtlety here. If she's an emotionally starved woman, she'll think, *Oh yeah, how long is this going to last.* The adage "actions speak louder than words" will put you on loudspeaker. Recount the little things you did when you first fell in love that she responded to favorably. Little things done consistently will get her attention. Patience with your strategy will bring you the rewards you seek!

Do these things as if your life depended on it, and remember time is of the essence.

Basically, get your act together. And be a man about it. When I say be a man about it, I mean you've got to pursue her as if you're pursuing a deer that doesn't want to be shot.

That assumes she's going to be running the other way. Maybe she's had-it-up-to-here with you and considers it over. Maybe she just wants to be pursued. Women want you to prove you want them and that they are worth wanting. It makes them feel worthy of the pursuit. So they may turn away from you hoping secretly that you'll keep knocking. If she slams the door in your face, hangs up on you, or just says, "I'm not interested," you've got to keep it coming. That's the manly thing to do.

If you give up too easily, what you're saying to her is that she's not worthy of pursuit or you're not man enough to go after her. Either way, you've just made yourself less desirable. But in everything there's a time to push and a time to back off and give her room. Sometimes it's good to express your intentions and then back off and let her have some time to reassess the situation. And just when she gets to wondering if you're going to make another go of it, you surprise her with a gallant effort.

Be careful not to be annoying to the woman who believes she knows "how you really are–the emotionally absent husband who must now have some ulterior motive." You must first swing the pendulum of experiences to the positive. When your wife sees you, what is the emotional response you get? Does she associate you with pleasure and happiness or pain and conflict? Her association with you will dictate how she views your actions. When you're together, make great effort for these moments to be happy.

I'm not saying these desperate measures will always work, but you have to try. Maybe she associates too much pain with you to even want to try to make it work. Maybe you just are not right for each other. Maybe YOU are better off without her. That said, most couples are well matched and the best thing they can do is repair what they have. Assuming neither of you is an alcoholic, drug addict, or psychopath, the problems can usually be worked out if you're both willing to take care of business and grow yourselves individually.

You know what all eight of Elizabeth Taylor's marriages had in common? Elizabeth Taylor! I'm not slighting Liz here, that's not the point. The point is that whatever is not working in your current relationship will probably not work in the next because YOU take YOU with YOU to the next one. Usually, if you fix YOU, you fix the problems. If you genuinely have fixed YOU and the relationship still doesn't fit, then by all means it's time for a new pair of shoes.

♥ Takeaways ♥

1. If your marriage is devoid of a healthy and satisfying sex life, you might just be asleep at the wheel and in need of a wake-up call.

2. You don't want to be one of those guys who wakes up with a cryptic note on his pillow that says, "Your breakfast is on the table. I hope you enjoy it because it's the last one I'll ever make you."

3. You never know where your mate's threshold of pain is. They don't know where it is. It's an invisible line that one only knows they've crossed once they've crossed it.

If any of this resonates with you, I suggest that you take immediate action to revitalize your relationship.

CHAPTER 9

THE BLUEPRINT FOR A LIFELONG LOVE AFFAIR

I feed my wife ice cream in bed every night.
— **Carl**, A seventy-six-year-old working electrician
when asked the secret to his great marriage.

L ove in marriage is without question life's greatest experience. We have glimpses into the spiritual domain whenever we experience love, whether with family, friends, children, or even the smile of a stranger. But is love enough to sustain a marriage? It's a loaded question. The answer stated elsewhere in the book is YES and NO. We're not concerned about just sustaining marriages here. We're interested in how to be mutually desired by one another so we can have a lifelong love affair. Right? Don't confuse love with "being in love." What we want you to experience is "being in love" now and forever.

If you are at all overwhelmed at this point, let me remind you that the rewards for loving your mate the way they need and want to be loved are immeasurable. There is no greater experience in this world than to have the all-out love, honor, respect, worship, and desire of the woman you love, worship, and adore. There is no greater pleasure than to share a deep, trusting physical connection with her that borders on spiritual. Yes, I am talking about sex.

As enamored and open as our society has become about sex, it still seems to be a difficult subject to talk about within a marriage. In fact, it is probably one of the most misunderstood subjects within a committed relationship due in part to a multitude of travesties. Religion has used doctrine regarding sex to influence behavior. Women have withheld sex as leverage to influence behavior. Parents have placed derogatory meanings on sex to influence behavior. But the biggest travesty of all is that people have been conditioned to believe that sex is optional in marriage. Well, it sure is optional if all you want is a partnership! However, sex is NOT optional if you want a healthy, God-intended marriage. When satisfying sex is absent for any significant period of time, your marriage can be on the rocks whether you know it or not.

Just How Important Is Sex?

So how much importance do you think polled couples place on sex in their marriages? Happy couples with good marriages say that sex only accounts for about 10 percent of what's important in their relationships. In contrast, unhappy couples in struggling marriages say that their sex life accounts for about 90 percent of what's wrong in their relationships. Wow! Do you think the quality of your sex life is important?

Modern couples must consistently "choose us" and put their marriages first. This doesn't just mean putting the romance and sex back into their marriages. It means consistently growing the quality of their connections, the quality of their behavior towards one another, and yes, the quality of their sex lives. By now you've figured out that sex is an important component of a marriage whether you feel like it or not. Just like eating, sleeping, bathing, caring for your children, and taking care of your responsibilities at work. You bathe and brush your teeth whether you really feel like it or not for many reasons. You have personal rules about hygiene; you don't want to offend anyone; you don't want to get cavities, etc. Likewise, you need to have rules and rituals in your marriage that keep you communicating, connecting, meeting each other's needs, and having quality sex.

There's no rule as to how often is too little or too much. It's about what meets the needs of your mate and keeps your intimacy alive as a couple. Three times a week or two times a month are both the right answer if that's what feels good for you both and helps you stay connected.

The Trifecta of a Lifelong Love Affair

Here's the plan that will give you the mate of your dreams, the marriage of your dreams, the sex of your dreams, and the life of your dreams. It takes love, commitment, and growing; but let me tell you, nothing is more worth the effort you will put into this. Nothing! Does that sound good? Let's do this!

Marriage Trifecta
DIAGRAM 1

Study Diagram 1 for a moment. What I most want to impress upon you is the dynamic and perpetual interplay between LOVE, ROMANCE, and SEX. Early on in a relationship your pursuit of your woman is linear. You want her, so you go through a charade of attracting her attention, pursuing her, romancing her, convincing her that you're a suitable mate, and then taking her off the market if she's willing. We call this process courtship. It's a progression that comes naturally to most people, albeit not always easily. The problems arise after marriage. Men think they've bagged the prize and that their job is done, that they can stop pursuing. Women also think that now that they've got their man they can let things go a little. Nothing could be further from the truth. Men and women both don't realize that the courtship process is perpetual if they want to have a passionate marriage that nurtures mutual attraction.

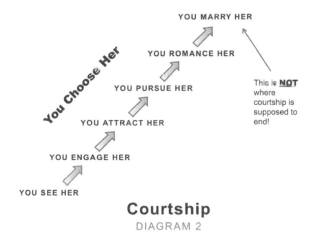

Courtship
DIAGRAM 2

Diagram 2 demonstrates the average man's view of courtship. You see what you want. You put on your A-game in pursuit of it, and you bag your prize. Job done! Right? Wrong!

The next illustration demonstrates more accurately how love, passion, attraction, romance, and sex are kept alive in a relationship. The trifecta of LOVE, ROMANCE, and SEX represents a perpetual interplay that goes on within a committed, passionate, growing marriage. Each feeds off the other. It's dynamic. It's a living organism. If you take one of these away, it's difficult if not impossible to sustain the others. If you don't have the trust and respect that's a part of love, it's difficult for her to want sex. If you're not having sex, it's difficult to feel loved and connected. If she doesn't feel adored through your romantic pursuit of her, she won't feel loved or have the desire for sex. If you aren't romancing her with focus and attention, you won't value her as a prize worthy of pursuit and she'll feel that.

At the beginning of marriage, love lays the foundation for everything to follow. However, as two people grow in love together, answering the question "What comes first?" becomes a moot point. Intimacy or sex? Love or romance? Sex or love? Each begets the other. Each nurtures and sustains the other, providing you with a perpetual source of energy.

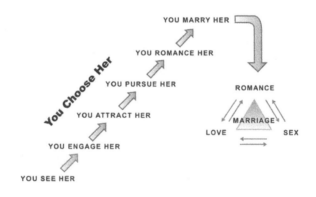

Courtship and Marriage
DIAGRAM 3

Great marriages don't just happen. They manifest as a result of approaching your relationship with intention and attention. Couples with passionate marriages "choose" each other on a daily basis. What I mean is that they give each other the gift of knowing they aren't there by accident or circumstance. It's letting your woman know she's the one you want and that she's worthy of your pursuit. It's showing her that she means enough to you that you're willing to continue improving yourself to be attractive to her. I don't mean just physical improvement. I mean mental, emotional, and spiritual improvement. It's giving her the gift of your presence—really being with her. A woman knows when you're present or distant when you're "listening" to her, embracing her, or having dinner with her. It's not enough to just focus on her nose! Being present is one of the greatest ways of demonstrating to anyone that they are

ROMANCE
- ✓PURSUIT
- ✓FOCUS
- ✓ATTENTION
- ✓TOUCH
- ✓COMMUNICATION
- ✓SPECIAL TREATMENT
- ✓EXCITEMENT
- ✓VARIETY
- ✓GIFT GIVING

MARRIAGE

LOVE
- ✓HONOR
- ✓RESPECT
- ✓COMPASSION
- ✓COMMITMENT
- ✓FORGIVENESS
- ✓PATIENCE
- ✓KINDNESS
- ✓PRESENCE
- ✓COMMUNICATION
- ✓SERVICE
- ✓PARTNERSHIP
- ✓MEETING YOUR LOVER'S NEEDS

SEX
- ✓CONNECTION
- ✓DEMONSTRATION OF LOVE
- ✓DEMONSTRATION OF COMMITMENT
- ✓TOUCH
- ✓COMMUNICATION
- ✓SPECIAL TREATMENT
- ✓EXCITEMENT
- ✓VARIETY
- ✓PASSION
- ✓POLARITY
- ✓SELF EXPRESSION
- ✓RECREATION
- ✓REJUVENATION
- ✓GROWTH
- ✓RELEASE
- ✓RESET

DIAGRAM 4

important to you, and it's a huge factor in building rapport and creating attraction.

When you study the components of the trifecta—LOVE, ROMANCE, and SEX—in Diagram 4 on the previous page, you'll not only see the interconnectedness of all three, but how all three are needed to fulfill the requirements of a great relationship and inspire the love affair of a lifetime.

So How Do Love, Romance, and Sex Happen in a Modern Marriage?

The answer is that you prioritize it. You schedule it. You integrate it. You bring it to the forefront of your consciousness. A great marriage is a "conscious" marriage. It means you live your marriage with intention and attention. However as life reveals its ugly head, the marriage we once enjoyed seems to slowly vanish like a mirage. The frequency and importance of real love, romance, and sex in our marriage diminishes as we reprioritize our life to incorporate careers and children. Sound familiar? Basically, we screw up our marriages for three distinctly different reasons.

1. We **trade** our marriages for the elusive American Dream by focusing most of our attention on "getting" things that in the end don't make us happy.
2. We **trade** our marriages for the "well-being" of our children.
3. We **trade** our marriages for a life of personal ignorance, stagnation, and entropy.

Let me explain. First, let's consider common yet infamous regrets of dying people. "I wish I had spent more time with my family." "I wish I didn't work so much." " I wish I had loved more." "I wish I had taken better care of myself." " I wish I had been a better husband/wife." These all demonstrate that we have bought into a big lie that our media and culture perpetuate. The lie is that status and possessions will make you happy. Keeping up with the Joneses is not just a cliché; it's part of our culture, both at work and at home. If we aren't working sixty-hour weeks, we get raised eyebrows from our colleagues and coworkers. We are an achievement-oriented society. We thrive on recognition and accolades and will make great sacrifices to experience them. Billionaire is the new millionaire, and every twenty-year-old with an above-average IQ expects to be the next one.

Over the last sixty years average home sizes and debt-to-income ratios have grown precipitously. We want everything! We want money, prestige, a big house, a second home, a sports car, and a boat. We want bragging rights. But at what cost? If you asked any married adult how important their marriage is to them, the answer would probably be "very important." However, most people do little or nothing to nurture and grow their marriage. Why? For one, we have been sold a bill of goods, and we have swallowed it hook, line, and sinker. We've focused too much on the wrong things and not enough on the things (read: people) that matter most. Another reason is that our society, our culture, and our educational systems have no built-in mechanism for growing a marriage. Nobody knows what to do. As a people we're generally clueless. As I stated in Chapter

1, it's like we've got a Ferrari in the garage but don't know how to use it.

The next bad trade we make is for our children. We'll do anything for our children, including compromise the most tangible example they have of what a marriage is supposed to be like. You think they don't notice? In case you're deluded, the kids don't come first. Let me repeat that. THE KIDS DON'T COME FIRST. That is the biggest childrearing philosophy pile-o-crap ever! People who say "the kids come first" have no marriage. That's why the kids come first. The kids are often a smokescreen for a mediocre relationship—just like the people who say "money is not important" usually have no money.

I've seen it time and time again; when a marriage is built on the foundation of raising children, and then suddenly the children are gone, there is nothing left to hold it together. The common thread is dissolved. Your marriage must be built on a foundation of love for each other. Children thrive when Mom and Dad are in love. They need to know it through your demonstration. It gives them a security and self-esteem that supports healthy development. It gives them positive expectations for their own love life. It gives them an example to strive for.

And finally, we trade our potential for a great marriage for a life of stifled personal growth. What people don't realize is that marriage is the primary mechanism humans have to facilitate personal development. That's why it is quite normal for marriages to have problems. Problems are just opportunities in disguise to grow as a couple into a more deeply rewarding experience. All your character flaws and damaged emotions are at some point confronted head-on. And when this happens, and trust me it happens, you are presented with an opportunity to grow as a human being or resist growth and cause yourself massive pain. These opportunities show up when your spouse is "rubbing you wrong," when you're in strong disagreement, when you have values conflicts, when you don't feel like your needs are being met, when your mate doesn't feel like her needs are being met, etc.

Personal growth happens when you are confronted with a problem and you overcome the problem, when you stretch yourself beyond your comfort zones. It happens when you "let go" of modalities that you think define who you are but really limit who you are. It means entertaining new paradigms for how to love and receive love. It's learning to love someone the way they need to be loved instead of how you want to be loved. It means letting go of old beliefs that inhibit you from really experiencing the juices of life. The opportunities for personal growth in your marriage are limitless and cannot be found in any other relationship.

In Chapter 1, I hypothesized that "women are God's mechanism for a man's ascension to godliness." The process of becoming the "husband of her dreams" parallels the path to righteousness. Marriage is the ultimate growing experience. In striving to be the husband a woman deserves, a man is forced to overcome his carnal tendencies that only exacerbate in the presence of only men. In a man's complete and total pursuit of his woman, he learns what it means to truly love; he learns to surrender "self"; he learns "mastery" over his emotions; and in experiencing her unveiling, he is revealed those attributes that only a woman can truly exemplify, including patience, compassion, and tenderness. Blasphemous? Hardly. Woman is man's perfect complement. She is the exemplification of everything that doesn't come natural to us as men. It's time to begin refocusing, realigning, and reprioritizing. Give your mate and yourself this gift and do it NOW.

Putting It All Together: The Plan

Here's the plan that will give you the mate of your dreams, the marriage of your dreams, and the sex of your dreams. By now you know that it takes love, commitment, and growing. When you wholeheartedly apply the insights I've shared, not only will your marriage be transformed, but your life will be as well. The influence that your marriage has on every area of your life is profound. Your physical well-being, your spiritual well-being, your financial well-being, and your career are all greatly influenced by the health of your relationship with your mate.

So here are three steps that will put you on the path of a great life.

Step 1: LOVE HER

Love your woman unselfishly and completely. To love your lady is to love her on her terms. Find out what her love language is and learn to speak it to her. You can't assume that what makes you feel loved is the same for your lady. In fact, I can guarantee that it is not. Here are things you can do to nurture and support love in your marriage.

1. First and foremost, always show up to your relationship in an empowered state. Consciously make sure that you have your A-game on. Remember that the quality of your relationship is a reflection of the quality of your state. When you are in a peak state, your capacity to be the man your woman needs is peaked. Your propensity to exude love, patience, and compassion is at a high. When you are in a peak state, you are unflappable. Your lady deserves your best. She needs your best.

2. Work to embody everything that love is and implies including honor, respect, patience, kindness, forgiveness, trust, compassion, commitment, and presence.

3. Support and fill your partner's needs. Make sure you know what their current versions of these needs are. This means you've got to ask them. You need to know what has to happen for her to feel loved. You need to know what has to happen for her to feel appreciated. You need to know what has to happen for her to feel significant. You need to know what has to happen for her to feel physically attracted to you. And remember, it doesn't matter whether you agree with what she needs or whether you share the same values. Her needs don't have to make sense. The secret is to find out what your woman wants/needs and then give it to her. Period! If you do this, you will own her! This is what it is all about. Sound good?

4. Keep the polarity alive. Celebrate your differences; focus on what's beautiful and ignore what irritates you.

Keep growing and evolving yourself as a human being and she will always be wondering what's around the next corner. Nurture those attributes in yourself that exemplify your manhood. Take control of your life and start getting things done. Get control of your finances, take your fitness level up a notch, and get that honey-do list caught up for once.

5. Have fun together. Fun is what you had before you got married. Having fun together gave you a positive association with each other, an association that compelled you to want to be together all the time. You've heard the old saying that "a couple that plays together stays together." It couldn't be truer.

6. Listen to her as if what she has to say is the word of God. It will show her that, in that moment, she is the most important person in your life. Giving anyone your undivided attention when they are talking to you is a great demonstration of respect and presence.

Step 2: ROMANCE HER

Most marriages are not lacking in love. They are lacking in the kind of love that distinguishes them from every other type of relationship—eros or erotic love. The chemicals our body produces during courtship and romance that are responsible for the euphoria we experience fade away after eighteen to twenty-four months. If we as men don't consciously work to keep romance alive, we'll eventually find ourselves with a frigid woman and an even colder bed. Here's what you need to do to keep the fire burning. This is not optional. This is a lifestyle!

Caveat: These suggestions presume that your lady is predominantly feminine. Always be sensitive to her reactions and make adjustments accordingly. This of course can be challenging given that women don't always know what they want and are often in denial as to what they really want. Just go with it.

1. Let her know she's the object of your desire. This must be done tastefully. Unless you have considerable rapport and trust in your relationship, telling her you think she is dripping hot and that you want to screw her brains out will probably be a turnoff.

2. Pursue her like she's a prize worth winning. Your lady needs consistent and perpetual validation that she's the woman you want. She needs fresh evidence that you love her. If you think for a second that you "have her" and that this is all a waste of time, you could be one of those guys that wakes up to a half-empty bed and a note on her pillow that says, "I'm finished."

3. Act as if she's the woman of your dreams and she will miraculously become the woman of your dreams.

4. Love her like a lover loves a lover.

5. Keep the flowers and gifts coming baby (assuming she responds favorably to this). Do it with variety, consciousness, intention and without a set schedule. You don't have to spend much time or money doing this. She just likes to know that you were thinking of her and took the time out of your schedule to do it.

6. Lovingly touch her throughout the day. Humans need touch especially from their mate. A touch, squeeze, hug, or kiss can convey feelings of love, compassion, attraction, connection, and gratitude.

7. Don't let chivalry die. Institute a higher code of conduct around your woman that makes her feel special. Open doors for her. Stand up for her when she comes to the table. Don't do things in her presence that you never would have done when you were dating. Show her the respect that a lady deserves. She might think you are being a little silly at times, but I guarantee that she'll like it.

8. Maintain an attractive appearance. Don't let yourself go. If you know she likes a clean-shaven face, make your best effort to look good for her. I'm certain you prefer her clean shaven. Am I right? Dress up for her once in a while even if it is at home.

9. Keep dating. If life is crazy, schedule a date night every week, kids or no kids. This is not optional. Go places you've never gone. Do things you've never done. You need to have this to look forward to.

10. Call her throughout the day like you used to just to see what she is doing or to hear her voice.

11. Tell her you think she's beautiful and mean it.

12. Tell her you can't stop thinking about her and mean it.

13. Mix it up. Don't fall into a predictable pattern in any of this. It's the unpredictability early on in a relationship that makes it so spicy and passionate. Don't smother her. Leave some space here and there.

You want to keep her guessing. However, the idea is to create a little uncertainty and anticipation without removing her security.

14. Nurture your polarity. Remember that a big reason men and women are attracted to each other in the beginning is their inherent differences. Many of those differences diminish over time as couples compromise and adopt each other's habits, tastes, preferences, and values. Therefore, it's imperative that you maintain a healthy sense of individuality and, as a man, masculinity. When it comes to romance, be a man about it. Take the reins and show her she's a prize worth having and that you're man enough to win it.

Step 3: SEX

Do I need to say more? Yes, I do. That's why I am devoting the next and final chapter to sex. The myths about sex that keep us from having it, why we need to have sex, and how to make sex happen are just a few of the topics covered. For the lucky few, sex is spontaneous and comes naturally. However, for many, sex is an awkward sticking point in their journey to a fulfilling marriage. Often, an individual's values and beliefs about sex become phantoms that interfere with their ability to have a gratifying and passionate sex life. We'll talk about these in the next chapter. In the meantime, here are the basics.

1. You need to be having sex. Sex is the primary thing that makes your relationship with your spouse unique from

all others. I'll suggest all the great reasons you need to be having sex in the next chapter.

2. Remember that sex is a byproduct of a great relationship.

3. Do it for each other even if you don't feel like it.

4. Have a weekly sex night or sex morning so that a week doesn't slip by without connecting with your lover in that way.

5. Throw in a quickie once in a while. Be spontaneous.

6. Endeavor to please your partner on a new level. Find out what their needs are and how they might not be being met, and start giving them what they want.

7. Don't ever feel like everything has to be perfect in your relationship to have sex. Sometimes sex can be the cure.

8. Do it with no expectations and pressure.

9. Schedule it. Something else has to give, period. A lot of people take offense to the whole concept of scheduling sex. They say that sex should be "spontaneous" and "uncontrived." I agree that spontaneous sex is great sex, however, those that "believe" (remember the power of beliefs and indoctrination?) sex should/must be spontaneous probably don't have any sex and their belief is probably why! What if the only time you had a great meal was when you spontaneously decided to cook and all the right ingredients just happened to be in the fridge? What if the only time you ever went to a great concert was when you just happened to be driving by a concert venue, saw a sign that Fleetwood Mac was playing in thirty minutes, and decided to go? Who would watch the kids? Is the time already blocked

out? Could you get tickets? No way! Point? Spontaneity is awesome, but not practical to wait for. I think we've got a new myth here to dispel.

Is spontaneous sex even the best sex? Not necessarily. Most of the memorable sex for me was planned. Think about it. Even when you were dating, the sex was planned. It just wasn't scheduled. Or was it? You often planned when you would be together, where you would go, what would happen afterwards. If it wasn't planned, it was anticipated. Right? When you want to have a phenomenal romantic dinner at home, what do you do? You choose the night and make sure it doesn't conflict with your wife's yoga class schedule, you identify the recipes you will use, you make a shopping list, you buy a good Cabernet, you set up the stereo to play your favorite jazz selection, etc. Alternately, if you want a great vacation, what do you do? You plan for it. You block out the time. You make flight reservations and hotel accommodations. You research all the possible activities you could engage in. Does all this planning make the vacation less desirable? No way! What it does is build anticipation for the event.

For a woman, planning for sex, anticipating sex, and preparing for sex can be the ultimate foreplay. The fact that it is scheduled in the midst of a hectic life is something to look forward to. The fact that you both know it is important enough to plan for in an otherwise crazy existence says a lot about how you value your relationship. Unless you are retired with no children living with you, waiting for sex to "happen" is like waiting to win the lottery to pay your bills. You'll just end up in marriage bankruptcy.

Wrapping it up

Don't take any of this too seriously. The formula for a great marriage is not a mathematical equation. It's much more fluid than that. Life is a dance. It's full of surprises, twists and turns, and constant challenges. While the principles shared in this book are tried and true, their application requires finesse and artistry. The best analogy I can think of for this is that of landing an airplane. The process (formula) for landing an airplane can be taught on a chalkboard or in the pages of a book. However, the application of the "formula" in practice takes artistry and finesse. It requires a pilot to be fully present and alert to the infinite variables that nature (life) tends to throw at him. As in flying, life and marriage are full of crosswinds, down drafts, and whole assortment of challenges that surprise us when we take our eye off the ball for just a little too long. Staying on course requires us to live fully in the moment and consistently make small corrections. And just when you think that you've got it mastered, it throws you a curveball.

There is no such thing in life as absolute perfect. Mastery is a process, not a destination. It's taking the knowledge and resources you have and applying them to the best of your ability so that you are always growing and challenging yourself to a new level. If you take from this book what resonates with you and apply it wholeheartedly, you too can be on the quest to make your marriage your life's greatest experience.

Well, we're just about done! However, now that we've got our lady up on a pedestal where she belongs and your desire for each other is building, we want to make sure we don't screw it all up in the bedroom. The next and final chapter debunks some of the myths (read: disempowering beliefs) people have about sex and reveals eleven really cool reasons you need to be having more of it.

♥ Takeaways ♥

1. The trifecta of LOVE, ROMANCE, and SEX represents a perpetual interplay that goes on within a committed, passionate, growing marriage. If you take one of these away, it's difficult if not impossible to sustain the others. If you don't have the trust and respect that's a part of love, it's difficult for her to want sex. If you're not having sex, it's difficult to feel loved and connected. If she doesn't feel adored through your romantic pursuit of her, she won't feel loved or have the desire for sex. If you aren't romancing her with focus and attention, you won't value her as a prize worthy of pursuit and she'll feel that. At the beginning of marriage, love lays the foundation for everything to follow. However, as two people grow in love together, answering the question "What comes first?" becomes a moot point.

2. Great marriages don't just happen. They manifest as a result of approaching your relationship with intention and attention. Couples with passionate marriages "choose" each other on a daily basis. They give each other the gift of knowing they aren't there by accident

or circumstance. It's letting your woman know that she's the one you want and that she's worthy of your pursuit. It's showing her that she means enough to you that you're willing to continue improving yourself to be attractive to her. I don't mean just physical improvement. I mean mental, emotional, and spiritual improvement. It's giving her the gift of your presence. A woman knows whether you're present or distant when you're "listening" to her, embracing her, or having dinner with her. Being present is one of the greatest ways of demonstrating to anyone that they are important to you, and it's a huge factor in building rapport and creating attraction.

3. When you study the components of LOVE, ROMANCE, and SEX in Diagram four, you'll not only see the interconnectedness of all three, but how all three are needed to fulfill the requirements of a great relationship and inspire the love affair of a lifetime.

CHAPTER 10

SEX 202
(Why You Need to Be Having Sex)

Every true lover knows that the moment of greatest satisfaction comes when ecstasy is long over and he beholds before him the flower which has blossomed as a result of his touch.

—Don Juan DeMarco

R eally? Do we really need coaching on sex? After all, we live in the age of enlightenment. Or do we? We actually live in the information age. It's not the same thing. Let me enlighten you about something. If you don't regularly describe your sex life using words like "amazing," "awesome," "indescribable," or "mind-altering" then you probably need to read this chapter. If your sexual experiences don't consistently leave you wondering why you don't do it more often, one or all of three things are getting in the way. First, you may have disempowering beliefs (myths) about sex; second, you may not realize the profound importance of sex in your marriage; third, you may not actually know what you are doing. So let's get down and dirty by first dispelling some commonly held myths about sex that can stymie your potential for a fulfilling sexual relationship and marriage.

Dispelling Myths about Sex

Myth is the most common word but really the wrong word to use in this context. They are really beliefs that may govern or influence the quality of your connection with your mate, the quality and frequency of sex—and they can ultimately screw up your life. Myths, in this context, are things we might believe to be true that in fact are detrimental to a healthy relationship and a healthy sexuality. It is my hope that if any of these are a part of your experience, you will at least entertain an alternative perspective and allow yourself the gift of new possibilities.

Myth #1

A great relationship has nothing to do with sex. True, if you're not married! A primary difference between a good friendship and a good marriage is sex. You don't need sex to be great friends. However, you must have sex, if not great sex, to have a great marriage.

Dr. Phil McGraw in his number one bestseller Relationship Rescue suggests that sex provides couples a respite from the rat race, a place they can go to relax, reconnect, and stay involved. He also adds that without sex your relationship is reduced to "one devoid of uniqueness."

Marriages with unsatisfying sex are more often than not on the road to alienation, infidelity, and divorce. Extramarital affairs happen not necessarily because of lack of love, but because of the absence of sex or, more poignantly, gratifying sex. Individuals going outside their marriage for sex usually aren't looking for love; rather they are looking to gratify an unmet need. That need usually takes form in the excitement and eroticism of being with someone who allows them to be sexually true to themselves without being judged.

Good sex is an integral part of a healthy marriage. A great marriage depends on an open, loving, and expanding sexual connection. Sex is a continual validation of the commitment made at the altar. It is an act of honoring your mate. It's a testimony that "today, I have once again chosen you." Sex is not optional. In fact, the Bible refers to it as "due benevolence."

First Corinthians 7:3-5 says:

Let the husband render to his wife due benevolence: and likewise also the wife to the husband. The wife has not power of her own body, but the husband: and likewise also the husband has not power of his own body, but the wife. Defraud not one another, except it is with consent for a time, that you may give yourselves to fasting and prayer; and come together again, that Satan tempts you not for your incontinency.

Sexual intimacy is a "conjugal duty" in a marriage. It is not optional. To deprive or deny your spouse of sexual fulfillment is to defraud them (biblically speaking). In other words, it's a breach of contract. When you got married, you promised each other that you would meet each other's needs and that your mate would not have to go anywhere else to have them met. It was not a conditional promise. Any questions?

Myth #2

Great sex just doesn't happen in a monogamous relationship. Not true! However, it's a rare experience. You know, sort of like seeing a comet or a lunar eclipse. It happens, just uncommonly. Why? Because we allow the minutia of our lives to distract us from what is really important. We stop treating our lover like a lover and everything goes to hell in a hand basket from there.

Great sex outside a committed relationship is an event. Great sex within a committed relationship is an experience that begins long before the act of sex and perpetuates long after. The alchemic interplay of love, romance and sex when cultivated in a monogamous relationship is kind of like getting to have all the cake and ice cream you want albeit it might be gluten and dairy free.

Why don't most couples experience this? The answers are in the previous pages so I won't repeat myself. However, one of the things I hope you will glean from this book is that the absolute BEST sex happens only in a monogamous relationship. Once you begin to coax the "goddess" out of your lady, you'll question who the weaker sex really is!

Myth #3

Sex is for procreation only. Sex is a gift given us by God. Sex, along with the power of choice and the ability to bring meaning to our lives, is what separates us from the animal kingdom. Putting these three together, we as human beings have the ability to choose to have meaningful sex. If it were only for procreation, God would not have given us desire, nor would she have made it pleasurable. For further study, see the appendix for additional materials on the role that religion has taken in robbing people of their God-given gift of sexuality.

Myth#4

Men want sex more than women. Another way of putting this would be that men are the more "high-desire" partner. This is a myth perpetuated by social pressure and the fact that both men and women, on average, have never felt comfortable expressing their true needs, desires, and problems because of that social pressure. Speaking in generalizations of course, if a man has low libido, he feels less "manly." His lack of sexual desire is a blow to his masculinity and not something he will readily admit, take responsibility for, seek help for, and certainly not share in a questionnaire. If a woman has a high sex drive and finds her needs consistently not being met, she's conditioned to keep her mouth shut. In high school, the high-desire girls were always "sluts." They're told that "guys are the ones that think about nothing but sex." Forget every preconception you may have. Every relationship has a high-desire and a low-desire partner, and it's not gender determined.

The high-desire partner in one relationship could be the low-desire partner in the next.

Myth #5

Sex is "dirty" or immoral. You're darn right it's "dirty"! If it's done right. Woody Allen says, "Sex is dirty, that's why you should save it for someone you love!" Well, in the context of swapping bodily fluids, I think he's right. When we talk about "monogamous f**king" in our bonus chapter, you really have to question the sanity of engaging in such an act outside of a monogamous relationship. So where is the myth? I think it ties in with Myth #3. The belief that sex is "dirty" from a philosophical standpoint is an indoctrination that some people have had instilled and perpetuated by their religion, their parents, their education, and social influences. It's an indoctrination just like the belief that money is the root of all evil, you should never talk to strangers, or you must go to college to succeed in life. These things are treated as absolute truths and influence our decision making and how we interpret the world around us.

The belief that sex is "dirty" has been perpetuated by fear rather than love. A parent's fear of a daughter getting pregnant. A husband's fear of a woman's overt sexuality. A church's fear of losing control over its members. Many churches use guilt to control their memberships by keeping them in a perpetual cycle of sin-guilt-repentance. Associating sex with sin and sin with guilt has made sex a "dirty" word. Certainly there is "dirty" sex, in the sinful sense of it, such as sex performed for money, sex that degrades human beings, sex that is used to control another, and sex that is manipulative. In an effort to prevent teen girls from doing something stupid, parents tell them things like, "If you have sex before you're married, no decent guy is going to want you." The message they get is that sex makes them unclean. What a travesty!

If you have moral hang-ups (religious beliefs) about sex or specific sexual practices that are barriers to a fulfilling sex life with your lover, please see the appendix for additional reading material on the subject. What if your beliefs about sexual immorality were based not on the Bible but on religious and social tradition? What if you learned that it is actually God's design for a husband and wife to experience each other's bodies without limits?

An all-you-can-eat buffet of sex between two consenting adults who love each other is one of the most beautiful things in the world, along with a baby being born, a desert sunset, and seeing two people in love. Whether it's "dirty" (morally and philosophically) or not, I think, is in the mutual intention of the two consenting adults doing it.

Myth #6

All men ever want is sex! It's the only thing on their minds.
This statement is false when men are in a mutually loving and engaging relationship. However, it is oftentimes very true when a marriage is cold, stale, and dispassionate and they're not "getting any." In other words, guys only obsess about sex when they aren't having enough of it. Otherwise,

they're thinking about cars, football, golf, fishing, making money, and, oh yeah, baby...how blessed we are to have YOU in our lives.

Myth #7

Intimacy increases desire. Not necessarily. Intimacy and passion are two different things. Intimacy and sensuality are two different things. Intimacy and sex are two different things. Intimacy does not beget desire. Intimacy begets connection, comfort, familiarity, and security. Intimacy is the experience of loving, sharing, knowing, and accepting. Intimacy can lead to the kind of sex one engages in to foster connection, reassurance, and love—all good things, but not desire. Not desire in the sensual, erotic sense as in "I want you!" You know, the kind of desire where you both start tearing your clothes off the second you see each other.

Sensual desire comes from liking what you see, being intrigued by what you see, being curious about what you don't see, and wanting a peek behind the curtain. It comes from getting a couple of licks of chocolate gelato and wanting more. Desire forms in the gap between what you take for granted and what is intangible. In other words, desire is the emotion you experience when you long for what you don't have, whereas intimacy comes from being secure in what you do have.

Myth #8

You both need to "be in the mood" to have sex. Another way of putting this is that all the planets need to be in alignment before sex can or should happen. This is one of the most destructive and sabotaging beliefs you can have. Modern marriages are fraught with challenges that couples didn't have in our parents' and grandparents' day. If the pressures of careers, child rearing, and finances aren't enough to quell sexual desire, then the inherent depolarizing of men and women in egalitarian marriages is sure to do the trick. If anything, you need to be having more sex for all the reasons listed below.

Reasons Why You Need Sex in Your Marriage

Do you need a reason to have sex? Well, there are more reasons than you probably guessed why you need sex in your life. What if you found out that your marriage depended on it? What if you found out that your health depended on it? As people mature in their relationships and get older, they often out of ignorance take for granted the role that sex plays in a healthy life. You are about to see just how key a role sex plays in maintaining your emotional, mental, and physical well-being.

Reason #1

Procreation. Okay, this is obviously optional. However, it is difficult for two committed people in love not to want to make babies.

Reason #2

Connection. The physical intimacy of sex uniquely connects you to your mate. This crazy world we live in with work, kids, schedules, household duties, and so forth all works to disconnect us from our lover. Making love is a great way to reconnect, reassure, and reaffirm the promises made in the beginning. Maybe, just maybe, if couples had more sex they would feel more connected instead of waiting to feel more connected to have sex.

Reason #3

Bonding. The intimate physical connection that comes through sexual intercourse bonds two people together as lovers and mitigates the propensity to look outside the relationship for fulfillment. The meeting of each other's sexual needs fulfills the pledge made at the altar. Marriage is the "act of uniting" as one. Sex is the physical declaration and affirmation of that.

Reason #4

Demonstration of love. Both men and women can use sex as a way to demonstrate their love and affection. It's a way of saying, "Baby, I love you and I don't want there to be any physical space between us. I want to make you feel good. I want to give you pleasure. I want you to know that you are the special person in my life." Sex is an active demonstration of commitment and surrender to each other. It's a gift of love to your mate and to yourself.

Reason #5

Act of devotion. Sex is a primary way in a marriage to demonstrate to our mate that we are theirs. It's an offering of ourselves that affirms the vows we took at the altar to give ourselves only to our beloved. In Tantra, this is known as divine union.

Don't underestimate the power of the Devotion as we like to call it. The Devotion is a weekly, if not daily, gift that we give each other. It ensures that we connect on an emotional and physical level (without any grandiose expectations) for a few minutes before we go to sleep each night. Many times, one of us is tired or mentally exhausted and not up for making love. However, the low-desire partner will almost always be happily willing to devote. It is relaxing and enjoyable, not vigorous or a commitment to fully engaged sex. It's an affirmation to each other that they mean the most to you and that you are not ignoring their needs. Often, though, it turns into much more than that. This ties directly into Myth #8.

Reason #6
Rejuvenation. Sex is good for the well-being of your marriage. It makes you feel good. It releases endorphins into your bloodstream. Sex can also feel cleansing by releasing pent-up energy and anxiety. As one husband aptly put it, "Sex gets the poison out."

Reason #7
Recreation. Sex is fun, or at least it should be. Couples that have fun together stay together. Your bodies are like an endless

playground of possibilities. Doesn't humping like rabbits sound more fun than going to the movies? Who says they have to be mutually exclusive?

Reason #8

Reset. Making love is a great way to periodically (daily, weekly, monthly) "reset" your relationship. Your coming together (no pun intended) in the bedroom is an expression and validation of every other reason listed here. It says, "I love you, We are good, Everything is okay, I'm here for you, You are still my special one, I choose you," etc.

Reason #9

Self-expression. Sex is an opportunity for individuals to take off the mask they wear in public and express the side of themselves that they suppress because of social norms. Social pressure, politics, and religious dogma all make it unacceptable for some people to be true to themselves. Proper gender roles as mandated by American society have precluded men, and more often women, from expressing their true sexuality overtly. Behind-closed-doors sex often provides people a canvas for self-expression and release. Sexuality, as with most things, can be expressed as an art form as exemplified in the Kama Sutra. Sometimes you might feel like who you or your lover are in the bedroom is incongruent with who you are in your public life. Not necessarily true. We all have many facets to our personalities. For every need to be harnessed, there is an opposite need to be unleashed. For every need to be in control, we have the need to be wild. For every need for structure, we have the complementary need for spontaneity. And for those tending towards the prudish or puritanical, there might just be a little Casanova dying to express himself.

Reason # 10

Longevity. Studies have shown that a happy marriage and a prolonged sex life are keys to longevity. People in love have higher levels of endorphins and lower levels of destructive lactic acid and cortisol. The challenges and strains of life are more easily endured with a mate to share the experiences with. Being loved releases oxytocin, known to reduce blood pressure. But more to the point, sex is a huge stress reliever and can factor significantly in the prevention of heart disease. Men also have a built-in need to ejaculate. A man's prostate produces semen most, if not all, of his life. If your prostate is producing semen, the semen needs to be regularly expelled and regenerated for the health of the prostate. Many doctors have concluded that prostate cancer could be largely mitigated by maintaining an active sex life into old age. The axiom "use it or lose it" holds true once again.

Reason #11

You're horny as hell and can't contain yourselves. You know how it is when you are tearing each other's clothes off in a fit of passion…right? Or does that only happen in the movies? I sincerely hope not. I'm talking about spontaneous "I want you right here and now" sex. No plan, no agenda, just unbridled primitive sex. It's when two people want to f**k and everything else just fades into insignificance.

A Little about the Process

This book is not about how to do sex. It's about how to keep the desire and passion alive and well. So, I'm going to give you some very general but noteworthy tips and call this chapter good. The truth is that if you can get the growth and relationship part of the equation on a roll, the "How to Have Sex" or even "How to Have Awesome Sex" part will take care of itself. There's not going to be any lessons on mechanics, anatomy, or best positions. However, you will find recommendations for further study in the appendix.

Here I would like to share a cheat sheet of tips I have learned from personal experience, extensive research on sex and human sexuality, and interviews with happily married couples. I share these because as "knowledgeable" and "experienced" as most people think they are, most are ignorant about something that inhibits truly fulfilling sexual experiences. Here goes:

1. **Relax and don't stress about it.** Sex is seriously important but not to be taken so seriously. It's about having fun and enjoying each other. It's a joyous act of giving and receiving, a celebration that you've once again chosen each other.

2. **Approach sex from the perspective of filling your lover's needs.** The most fulfilling sexual encounters are often those with no expectations for oneself. Approaching your lovemaking from the perspective of loving, serving, and gratifying your lover can manifest real magic.

3. **Always be a willing and grateful (guiltless) recipient of pleasure.** Some people feel guilty receiving pleasure and have a hard time relaxing. Men in particular can suffer from premature ejaculation solely from the anxiety and fear of "cumming" too soon. Ironic, huh? One of the greatest gifts you can give your lover is graciously allowing him or her to give you pleasure without concern of having to immediately return the favor. That's supposed to be part of the beauty of marriage, knowing that you have a lifetime together to explore, expand, and indulge yourselves in the sensual pleasures reserved for loving, committed, consensual adults.

4. **Never pressure your partner to do something they are uncomfortable with.** This is a deal breaker. A marriage by definition is a loving, patient, and committed environment that in a healthy evolution will grow to encompass all that really matters. If you think that in order for you to have a good time your wife has to take it in the tail or let you "cum" on her face, you've been spending way too much time watching porn and not enough time really loving your wife. A word to the ladies: if your husband is making requests that are way out of your comfort zone, he's probably not getting enough sex and is using porn as an outlet. A word to both men and women: if your idea of good sex is the missionary position with the lights off, you're both in need of a boost in imagination and personal growth. Please see the appendix for recommended reading.

5. **Always have good personal hygiene.** Bad breath or body odor can really spoil a good time. For planned sex, it's great to have a pre-sex hygienic preparation ritual. Not only does it get the body ready, it helps get the mind ready, which in turn, for women, helps get the body ready.

Gals (and Guys in principle): Make it a point to always look your best for your lover. Wear your nice clothes at home. Put on his favorite heels and keep your toes freshly painted if you know he likes that. It's important to be visually stimulating and keep his attention. That's part of the polarity that attracted you together in the beginning. But don't stop there. I think it's important to feel good, smell good, and taste good too! Don't you think?

6. **Guys: Remember—she always comes first!** No pressure here, right? The average guy can go from arousal to climax to loss of erection in 2.8 minutes flat. It takes a woman 13 minutes (10 minutes longer) on average to reach climax. This assumes that you have skills and know where your lady's buttons are. Learn to delay your climax until she has had at least one. You'll both enjoy each other much more. After all, it's all about the journey, not the destination. Right? See appendix for additional ideas and resources.

7. **Guys: Become a cunnilinguist.** Look it up if you have to.

You always were a cunning linguist, James.
— **Moneypenny** to James Bond, ***Tomorrow Never Dies***

8. **Gals: He needs to know what works for you and what doesn't.** Every woman is different. What feels good to you changes. He can't possibly keep up with it without your loving guidance. Softer, firmer, lower, or "do it like this" really, really helps. When you're both focused on each other, a loving union will be a natural progression. However, for you to have the ultimate experience, communication on what feels good is needed. Heaven forbid you miss out on these experiences because you have not opened channels for direction.

If you're applying the tips and techniques throughout this book, your mind will already be prepared and great lovemaking will be anticipated. The mental component is 90 percent of what is needed to experience great sex.

Also, a great loss for you both is for your partner to think you're enjoying yourself when you're not. He can't know unless you tell him, and "faking" isn't a favor to either of you.

Once you learn to focus (easier with your eyes open) on your partner, the transition into the present moment will be easy, and the experience will be incredible. You really don't want to miss out!

9. **Never criticize your partner during sex.** Implied criticism comes in many forms, and it can bring desire to a screeching halt. If something makes you uncomfortable or turns you off, there's a way to lovingly, if not jokingly, let your lover know. However, there is a time and season for everything, and some things are just never in season. If you tell your wife you don't like the way she does her hair while she's giving you "head," you can forget about a blowjob for a long time.

10. **Guys and gals: Quickies are good.** But "longies" are better. Fitting in sex whenever or wherever possible is fun, necessary, and sometimes the best you can do. But it doesn't replace the importance and necessity of planned quality, intimate time together.

11. **Forget what you've seen in porn.** Women are getting paid to pretend they enjoy stuff that doesn't necessarily feel good to them. Porn can be detrimental to the outcome of sexual encounters in that men who indulge in it come to the bedroom with expectations that aren't shared by their wives. If porn is watched, it should be watched together and used as a tool for mutual fun, excitement, and to spark the imagination.

12. **Guys: The time to start getting her in the mood for more sex is after you've just had sex.** For many guys, their outward displays of affection and sensitivity drop

off appreciably after sex. That's the time for you to "grow up" and give her the same attention and regard you did leading up to the big event. If you really want to impress her, give her après sex romance that continues up to the next encounter and beyond.

13. **Guys: If you can't get it up, get help.** I don't care how old you are. It's not something to be ashamed about. If your heart stops working correctly, you go get a pacemaker, right? Just another note: If your twig is permanently retired for whatever reason, that doesn't mean your lover's needs should go unmet. You don't have to use a penis to have sex. God forbid your woman suppresses her sexuality because your noodle went limp. Another note to you older guys: just because you may not desire sex doesn't mean your honey doesn't. She puts dinner on the table for you whether she's hungry or not. Savvy?

14. **Sex is like cooking.** If you eat the same thing all the time, it gets kind of boring. You buy cookbooks to keep things interesting in the kitchen, right? Likewise, there are infinite recipes for sharing physical intimacy. Sometimes you need a little help with ideas. How about sex in the kitchen and dinner in bed? See the appendix for "interesting" books.

15. **Great monogamous sex begins outside the bedroom.** It's referred to as "making love all the time." Ever feel like foreplay is a formidable task? Foreplay, which should be likened to fanning a flame, has become for some more like building a fire with a flint and steel.

Making love all the time keeps the ember alive, ready to burst into flame with the least prompting.

16. **Slow down!** Sex is not a race to orgasm. Sex is a gift that is an unfolding journey and not a destination. If sex for you is just about relieving yourself of some pent up pressure with a few minutes of thrusting followed by 3-5 seconds of spasmodic relief, then relationship is probably not for you.

Learn to just be with each other; letting go of any premeditated outcome. Great sex is being fully present. It happens when you are truly being with someone and there is no desire to be anywhere else. Great sex is loving, knowing, learning, exploring, trusting, trying, submitting, asking, giving, receiving, growing, and evolving.

How good can your health be if you subsist on primarily fast food? By the same token, how good can your relationship be if sex is a 7-10 minute purely physical experience? For you, it might be enough. For your lady, I can almost guaranty that it is dissatisfying and disappointing.

If a woman doesn't want to have sex, it is often because she finds it so disappointing that she would rather do the dishes instead. She would rather suppress or deny her natural desire than subject herself to merely being an instrument of an insensitive man's temporary pleasure.

What a woman wants is a lover's touch. She wants to feel as though your fingers are memorizing her form as if you are experiencing it for the first time or even perhaps the last. She wants to feel as if her body is a canvas being colored by the brush strokes of an artist. She wants to feel as if she is a fine instrument being coaxed to reveal her inner music. She wants to feel the heat of your attention and your presence. She wants to feel honored, pursued, coaxed, admired, appreciated and wanted as if she is the only woman in the world. She wants to be touched like a lover touches a lover.

As it is in the bedroom, so it is in the rest of your relationship. The quality of your lady's sexual experience and connection with you is usually a reflection of the overall quality of your marriage. An extraordinary sex life with your mate is indicative of having met her emotional needs on a deep level.

Okay folks, there you have it. All this writing about sex has me imagining my wife in her cowgirl chaps with nothing else on. So I am out of here.

But first, I want to congratulate you for getting this far and for taking this first step towards mastery in your marriage and your life. I hope to see you at one of our transformational marriage retreats or in one of our virtual support programs. My goal is for your experience to eventually become as effortless as possible so that this all becomes an easily sustainable experience. It's all really very simple. Everything in this book can be distilled down to just one thing: LOVE. Develop the pattern of thinking, behaving, and acting in a spirit of love. Love your lover like a lover loves a lover and your lover will be your lover. It may require you to stretch, to forgive, to grovel, to change, to grow, to evolve as a human being. But after all, that's what marriage is good for. If its true nature is discovered and nurtured, it's also the most profound experience of one's life. There is no greater pleasure than to share a deep, trusting, physical connection with your mate. It is my hope and prayer that you too can enjoy a taste of what can only be described as life's ultimate experience.

♥ Takeaways ♥

1. If your sexual experiences don't consistently leave you wondering why you don't do it more often, one or all of three things are getting in the way. First, you may have disempowering beliefs (myths) about sex; second, you may not realize the profound importance of sex in your marriage; third, you may not actually know what you are doing.

2. Any belief that keeps you from having an exciting and fulfilling sex life needs to be evaluated on the merits of the "fruit" that it bears. If the belief does not serve you in enriching your sex life, then by all means throw it out and adopt something that serves you.

3. There are too many reasons that the quality of your marriage depends on sex to not be enjoying it frequently. If you share these reasons with your lady, you might just start wondering how much is too much!

4. SLOW DOWN!

P.S. I have a bonus chapter titled "A Mind Blowing Peek into Super Hot Monogamy" available for the properly initiated. If you think you qualify, please go to: www.greatmarriagegreatlife.com/bonus-chapter.html

ABOUT THE
AUTHOR

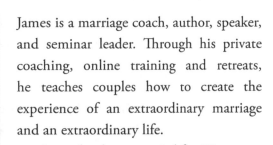

James is a marriage coach, author, speaker, and seminar leader. Through his private coaching, online training and retreats, he teaches couples how to create the experience of an extraordinary marriage and an extraordinary life.

James has been married for 27 years to Kimberly, his high school sweetheart. When he is not working at changing the world one marriage at a time, he can be found enjoying the outdoors on his mountain bike, or occasionally behind a ski boat. James lives with his family somewhere in the mountains near Boulder Colorado.

ADDITIONAL RESOURCES

Relationships and Intimacy

Chapman, Gary D., Dr. *The 5 Love Languages: The Secret to Love That Lasts*, Northfield Publishing, 2015.

Deida, David. *The Way of the Superior Man: A Spiritual Guide to Mastering the Challenges of Women, Work, and Sexual Desire.* Sounds True, 2004.

Evans, Jimmy. *Lifelong Love Affair: How to Have a Passionate and Deeply Rewarding Marriage.* Baker Books, 2012.

Gorga, Melissa. *Love Italian Style: The Secrets of My Hot and Happy Marriage.* St Martin's Press, 2013.

Gottman, John M. *The Seven Principles for Making Marriage Work.* Harmony, 1999.

Gray, John. *Men Are from Mars, Women Are from Venus: The Classic Guide to Understanding the Opposite Sex.* HarperCollins, 2004.

Haltzman, Scott. *The Secrets of Happily Married Men: Eight Ways to Win Your Wife's Heart Forever.* Jossey-Bass, 2007.

Harley Jr., Willard F. *His Needs Her Needs: Building an Affair-Proof Marriage*. Revell, 2011.

Hendrix, Harville and Hunt, Helen Lakelly. *Making Marriage Simple: 10 Truths for Changing the Relationship You Have into the One You Want*. Crown Publishing Group, 2013.

Morris, Howard J. and Lee, Jenny. *Women Are Crazy Men Are Stupid: The Simple Truth to a Complicated Relationship.* Gallery, 2010.

Penner, Clifford and Joyce. *The Married Guy's Guide to Great Sex: Building a Passionate, Intimate, and Fun Love Life*. Tyndale House Publishers, 2004.

Perel, Esther. *Mating in Captivity: Unlocking Erotic Intelligence*. Harper Perennial, 2007.

Roberts, Ted and Roberts, Diane. *SEXY Christians: The Purpose, Power, and Passion of Biblical Intimacy*. Baker Books, 2011.

Schnarch, David. *Passionate Marriage: Keeping Love & Intimacy Alive in Committed Relationships*. W.W. Norton & Co., 2009.

Sexless Marriage

Davis, Michele Weiner. *The Sex-Starved Marriage: Boosting Your Marriage Libido: A Couples Guide*. Simon & Schuster, 2004.

Schnarch, David. *Resurrecting Sex: Solving Sexual Problems & Revolutionizing Your Relationship*. Harper Perennial, 2003.

Romance

Corn, Laura. *101 Nights of Great Romance*, Kindle Edition, 2012.

Cronin, Stan. *How to Date your Wife*

Sex and Morality/Sex and Spirituality
Deida, David. *Finding God through Sex: Awakening the One of Spirit Through the Two of Flesh.* Sounds True, 2005.

Deida, David. *Enlightened Sex: Finding Freedom & Fullness Through Sexual Union.* Sounds True, 2004.

Pilkington, Clyde L. *Due Benevolence: A Survey of Biblical Sexuality.* Bible Student's Press, 2010.

Roberts, Ted and Roberts, Diane. *Sexy Christians: The Purpose, Power, and Passion of Biblical Intimacy.* Baker Books, 2011.

Tantric Sex, Sexual Fun and Technique
Corn, Laura. *101 Nights of Great Sex: Sealed Secrets. Anticipation. Seduction.* Park Avenue Publishers, 2013.

Chia, Mantak and Maneewan and Douglas, Abrams and Rachel. *The Multi-Orgasmic Couple: Secrets Every Couple Should Know.* HarperOne, 2002.

Daffner, Diana. *Tantric Sex for Busy Couples. How to deepen your passion in just ten minutes a day.* Hunter House, 2009.

Kerner, Ian. *She Comes First: The Thinking Man's Guide to Pleasuring a Woman.* William Morrow Paperbacks, 2009.

Kingsley, Eve. **Just F*ck Me: What Women Want Men to Know About Taking Control in the Bedroom.** Secret Life Publishing, 2011.

Lacroix, Nitya. *The Art of Tantric Sex: Ancient Techniques & Rituals that Enhance Sexual Pleasure.* DK Adult, 2006.

THE MARRIAGE MASTERY CLUB
ONLINE COUPLES TRAINING

Turn your marriage around faster than you ever thought possible. This multi-module online coaching program will teach you what everyone should have learned before they ever got married. If you want to re-ignite the ATTRACTION and PASSION in your relationship and FIRE THINGS UP in the BEDROOM, then this program is for you. In The Marriage Mastery Club video training series, you will find out how you can take INFIDELITY and DIVORCE completely off the table. If you have ever wondered what Happily Married Couples know that miserable couples don't and are ready to take your own relationship up a few notches, join the Marriage Mastery Club now.

Go to www.greatmarriagegreatlife.com for more information.

MARRIAGE MASTER CLASS
ELITE COUPLES RETREAT (3-DAY EVENT)

Marriage Master Class is total immersion into "Life's Most Enriching Experience." Why are so few couples able to experience a passionate, enduring marriage? Maybe you want to reignite the passion you once had. Are you looking for a "last-ditch" effort before you enter the big "D"? Is your sex life all but nonexistent? What if you could turn your marriage into your life's greatest and most rewarding experience? If you're tired of settling for less than a passionate and fulfilling relationship, then MMC is your program. What might your future look like if you don't turn things around now? Don't let another year, or even worse, 5-10 years go by without giving yourself the gift of an extraordinary marriage and the life that you deserve. MMC is the hands-on college course we all needed to take before we got married. It will inspire you with new paradigms, new beliefs, and new skill sets that will transform your marriage and your sex life. When you leave MMC, your relationship will be on track to be hotter and more alive than ever before. Join James and Kimberly Horning and their field experts at this one-of-a-kind event in select locations.

To learn more about this life changing program, go to www.greatmarriagegreatlife.com.

9 781630 476748